THE
DIVORCE
SURVIVAL
GUIDE

THE
DIVORCE
SURVIVAL
GUIDE

*The Roadmap for Everything
from Divorce Finance to Child Custody*

CALISTOGA
PRESS

For general information on our other products and services or to obtain technical
support, please contact our Customer Care Department within the United States at
(866) 744-2665, or outside the United States at (510) 253-0500.

Calistoga Press publishes its books in a variety of electronic and print formats. Some
content that appears in print may not be available in electronic books and vice versa.

ISBN: Print 978-1-62315-379-3 | eBook 978-1-62315-380-9

Contents

Introduction

Whether or not you were the one to initiate a divorce, you're now committed to a major life change—one that will likely alter your living situation, your relationships with friends and relatives, and the time you have with your children. Divorce is never easy, but if you arm yourself with knowledge and understand the essential steps you must take to protect yourself, moving forward can be just a bit easier.

This book provides the information you need to understand the divorce process in the United States—from an overview of the legal procedures that are used throughout the court system to the kinds of things you will need to do to extricate yourself from your marriage. It also tells something of a cautionary tale, detailing what you can do to protect yourself from the games that spouses sometimes play to get whatever property and custody they feel they deserve.

The federal government leaves divorce up to the states, so every state in the country has its own divorce laws. At the back of this book, you'll find resources that provide overviews of the laws in all fifty states, which will help you navigate quickly to the information you need to begin your divorce process. If the state laws do not make sense to you, consult a legal professional.

While this book is not a substitute for legal counsel—nor does it provide legal advice—it does provide sound, practical information about mediation and attorneys, protecting your children, the kinds of legal questions to expect, and tools you can use to get yourself through the divorce process and start your new life.

Your emotional well-being is every bit as important as your financial and parental stability, and this book provides some perspective to help you understand the emotional hurdles you are about to surmount. The better prepared you are for what's ahead, the better you will be able to overcome it and the better your footing will be when you begin your new, single life.

PART ONE

Divorce 101

CHAPTER ONE

Taking the First Steps

You've just made one of the most difficult decisions of your life: You and your spouse are getting a divorce. Perhaps you made this decision by yourself months or even years ago, but now your cards are on the table and you're ready to move ahead. Or perhaps your spouse made the decision, and now you're shaken, feeling betrayed and alone when you thought you'd both made a lifetime commitment. Regardless, once you and your spouse have agreed to divorce, just about everything in your relationship will change. You may have lost trust and respect for your spouse, and there may be wounds—from infidelity, abuse, continuous conflict, or abandonment—that will take years to heal, if they can heal. It's hard to imagine that a greater challenge than deciding to divorce may be in your future, but sometimes that can be the case.

Holding on to your self-esteem and keeping your priorities in order can be extraordinarily difficult as you go through the legal process of divorce. You and your spouse will each come away with only part of the belongings and treasures you shared as a couple. You may need to sell your home and leave a neighborhood you know well, and your standard of living may become lower than the one to which you've become accustomed. The practical considerations may overwhelm the emotional ones in fairly short order, and while divorce is rarely pleasant, it can be the beginning of a new life.

I Want a Divorce—What Now?

The legal process of divorce will be uncomfortable at best and contentious at worst, and it will have an effect not only on you and your spouse, but also on your children, your family, and your friends. Most importantly, divorce will change the relationship you have with your spouse forever; if you have children together, you will continue your relationship in one form or another for the rest of your life. While this can all seem daunting, know that you are not alone. The United States has the sixth-highest divorce rate in the world, according to statistics gathered by DivorceRate.org.

American divorce rates are much higher for couples who marry in their teens or early twenties, with rates as high as 36 to 38 percent for couples who are twenty to twenty-four years old on their wedding day. Rates drop remarkably for couples who marry in their thirties: only 5 to 6 percent of couples who marry when they are thirty-five to thirty-nine years old get divorced, while 8.5 to 11.6 percent of couples who marry in their early thirties eventually split. While media outlets regularly report that 50 percent of all marriages in America end in divorce, this figure has dropped significantly over the last several years, coming in closer to 41 percent in 2012.[1]

Wherever you and your spouse fall in this spectrum, you will become part of a long tradition of ending marriages within the American legal system.

How to Prepare for the Divorce Process

While your marriage has been about love, communication, building a life together, passion, and raising children—at least it was in the beginning—your divorce will be about money, property, and custody. This is the reality of the legal system, and it can be a painful one, especially if

....

1. U.S. Census Bureau, "Marriages and Divorces—Number and Rate by State: 1990 to 2009," Table 133 in *Statistical Abstract of the United States: 2012,* http://www.census.gov/compendia/statab/2012/tables/12s0133.pdf.

you're feeling the wrenching emotions that come with a spouse's surprise announcement that your marriage is over.

Once you and your spouse have agreed to divorce, things will begin to change very quickly. It's likely that you will feel overwhelmed by all the paperwork and shifts in your living situation, and concerns for your children and property will flood into your life. Start making lists of things to do, and carry a small notebook so you can write down all the details as they pop into your mind.

To protect your own interests and shield yourself from the potentially contentious discussions you have ahead of you, take steps immediately to get your financial records in order. (You will find a complete checklist of financial documents at the end of chapter 4.) Rest assured that your spouse is doing the same.

From this point forward, you will have information that you must keep from your spouse. You will need to compile a lot of documents, and you need somewhere to store them instead of in your own home: consider a parent's house, your best friend's house, or your office or place of business if you work outside your home. If you have nowhere else to store them, get a safe-deposit box in a bank—not a box you share with your spouse, but one of your own. This might seem overly cautious, but even if you intend for your divorce to be short, friendly, and cooperative, it's always best to be prepared.

The First Ten Steps

Regardless of whether you are in control of the decision to divorce, if you and your spouse came to the decision together, or if you are on the receiving end of the news, this list will help you put things in place to protect both yourself and your assets.

1. **Make your children your top priority.** If you have children, they will be affected significantly by your divorce—a fact that can't be set aside or ignored. Think now, before things become particularly uncomfortable around your house, about the steps you need to take to maintain as much normalcy as possible in their daily lives. Routine can be stabilizing, and seeing you at their extracurricular

events or sharing time with you on a regular schedule will help make the divorce proceeding less terrifying and disruptive to them.

2. **Get a copy of your credit report.** You need to know exactly where all the family's money is, as well as what charges are being made to the family credit cards. If your spouse has been responsible for making the monthly payments to the credit cards, the mortgage company, and so on, you need to monitor these accounts to be sure that these payments continue. You also need to know immediately if your spouse attempts to get credit using your name.[2]

3. **Talk to an attorney.** You may not need to hire one just yet, but you need the expertise of someone who handles hundreds of divorce cases every year. An attorney in your area will know all the state laws and will be able to give you real information about your legal rights, especially in terms of your living situation and custody of your children. You want to be sure to avoid any errors that could jeopardize your ownership of your home or any other property, so the sooner you find out what the law requires in your state, the better.[3]

4. **Open your own checking and savings accounts.** If you don't already have an account in your own name, open one as soon as you can, so you can keep your own money separate from your spouse's funds. This is where you will put the money you will save for legal fees, allowing you to proceed with the divorce even if your spouse has control of all the money in your family's name. Use a different bank from the one that holds your family accounts, change the direct deposit of your paychecks to this account, and keep money here for your living expenses.

....

2. Jeffrey A. Landers, "9 Critical Steps Women Should Take to Prepare for Divorce," *Huffington Post*, March 3, 2011, http://www.huffingtonpost.com/jeffrey-a-landers /9-critical-steps-women-sh_b_828841.html.

3. Debra J. Braselton, "Ten Things You Need to Do If Divorce Is Imminent," Family -Law-Illinois.com, accessed January 14, 2014, http://www.family-law-illinois.com /Divorce/Things-You-Need-To-Do-If-Divorce-Is-Imminent.shtml.

5. **Apply for a credit card in your own name.** Having your own credit card will allow you to begin to reestablish your own credit separate from your spouse. It's also important to close joint credit accounts to keep your spouse from running up big charges that you may be responsible for later. If you can't close the accounts without your spouse's cooperation, alert your credit card companies to the change in your relationship so the account will be flagged should your spouse start making major purchases.[4]

6. **Get a post-office box.** Change your mailing address to a post-office box and have your mail forwarded to it. You will hold the only key, so there is no chance that your spouse will be able to access your mail. Here you can receive legal documents and other papers from your attorney, your own bank and credit card statements, and any other correspondence that relates to your investments and other assets.[5]

7. **Get your financial records in order.** These are the records you will keep at your parents' or a friend's home (or in a safe-deposit box). You will need a copy of your joint tax returns, proof of your income and your spouse's income, a copy of your mortgage agreement, copies of all your family's bank and credit card statements, evidence of major joint purchases, the lease or purchase information for your car, and many other documents. (See the checklist at the end of chapter 4).[6]

8. **Change your will and your living will.** Chances are that your spouse is the executor of your will, and he or she may be the sole beneficiary of your estate. You don't want that anymore, so make this change a top priority. Likewise, if you have an advance directive for your health care, your spouse is probably the person listed to make life-and-death medical decisions for you. While most states do not allow you to remove your spouse from your will until

....

4. Landers, "9 Critical Steps."

5. Ibid.

6. "How to Protect Your Assets in the Event of a Divorce," FeldLawBoston.com, accessed January 10, 2014, http://www.feldlawboston.com/Family-Law/How-To -Protect-Assets-in-Divorce.aspx.

your divorce is final, you can change the person listed to make medical decisions for you right away.[7]

9. **Change your beneficiaries.** Your spouse is undoubtedly the beneficiary on your insurance and investments, so you will need to change these right away as well. If you want to be sure that your children receive appropriate support in the event of your death, make them the beneficiaries. Some insurance companies will send notification to the previous beneficiary, so talk to your insurance company about your situation before you move ahead with the change, especially if you have not yet told your spouse about your plans for divorce.

10. **Collect information on your spouse.** If you are leaving your spouse because of his or her infidelity, abuse, financial irresponsibility, abandonment, alcoholism, or drug abuse—or any other reason beyond a basic inability to get along—you need to be ready with evidence if you need to defend your decision in court. Collect arrest records, correspondences, bank statements, photos, evidence of gambling debts, and any other evidence you have of your spouse's illegal, inappropriate, or adulterous behavior. Keep all this in a safe place outside your home—with the records discussed earlier—until you can turn it over to your attorney.

Divorce Q&A

Here are answers to a number of common questions posed by people going through divorce.

Q: My spouse has filed for divorce. What do I do?

A: Consult an attorney as soon as you possibly can. Based on the reason your spouse has given for the need to divorce you, you may need to defend your rights to property or custody of your children.

....

7. Landers, "9 Critical Steps."

You also may need to file a countersuit to gain custody rights, child support, alimony (or to contest alimony), and division of property. If you do not contest or file a countersuit, the case can be decided without your participation—meaning you will be bound by the judge's decision. Act promptly if you wish to contest or countersue, because once a judgment is filed, you have no further claim to anything that has been granted to your ex-spouse.

Q: What is a legal separation?

A: A legal separation is a court order that permits two spouses to live apart while they are still legally married. If there are children, the court will determine appropriate child custody and visitation schedules for the period of the separation, including child support payments to the spouse who maintains primary custody (the custodial spouse). In some states, a legal separation is required for a period of time—usually a year—before the marriage can end in divorce. The separation agreement protects both spouses from accusations of desertion or abandonment (both of which can be grounds for divorce) and allows one spouse to move out of the home without losing the right to that property.

Q: What is a dissolution?

A: In some states, a marriage can be ended legally with a dissolution, which can eliminate much of the time and expense of a divorce. Often called a "no-fault divorce," dissolution requires both spouses to come to an agreement about child custody, parental rights, visitation, support payments—including alimony—division of property, and payment of attorney fees. The two spouses must be willing to exchange information without the use of subpoenas. If both spouses are cooperative, the agreement is filed with the court and a hearing takes place in a fairly short time, conceivably within three months. The marriage can then be terminated in the hearing.

Q: What is an annulment?

A: An annulment is a legal determination that a marriage never occurred. It applies retroactively to the marriage, meaning that the marriage is considered invalid from the beginning. Annulment is very rare, and courts usually only issue them in cases of bigamy, incest, when one of the parties is below the legal age of consent, or when one of the parties is not of sound mind. The Catholic Church, which does not believe in divorce, can grant an annulment to members of the church if it determines that one of the two parties did not consent to the marriage.

Q: How long does divorce take?

A: This depends on a lot of variables. The more you and your spouse can agree on the division of your assets and property before you begin divorce proceedings, the more quickly the process will go. The timing will also be influenced by the backlog of cases in your county. In some states, you and your spouse are required to live apart for one year before you can file a request for divorce.

Q: Can I get a faster divorce on the Internet?

A: Probably not. Online divorce purveyors provide basic forms that allow you to file for divorce if both you and your spouse are in complete agreement about the division of your assets and the custody of your children. This is essentially the same thing as a dissolution, for which you must fill out forms and file them with the court in your county. Once the forms are filed, the timing will be the same whether you use an online service, work with an attorney, or fill out and file the papers with no legal help or advice. Online services do not provide legal counsel, so if you and your spouse disagree about any aspect of the division of property or child custody, the online route is not ideal.

Q: What will divorce cost?

A: There is no hard-and-fast rule for this, but an uncontested divorce (see chapter 2) can be completed for less than $1,000 if you and your spouse can come to an agreement on all terms without the use of attorneys. Your costs will include court filing fees and perhaps the use of a mediator who can help you reach agreements. If you must hire attorneys and enter into litigation to solve issues like child custody or division of property, your costs will go up significantly.

Q: What if I haven't been earning an income?

A: If you have been supported entirely by your spouse and you have no savings of your own, a divorce puts you at risk. You may be at a serious disadvantage when you need to hire an attorney, or when it's time to establish your own living situation. Legal fees, court costs, and bills for therapy can mount up very quickly, and you will need cash for a security deposit on an apartment as well as for rent and living expenses. If you are thinking about divorce but have not discussed it with your spouse, start putting aside whatever money you can as soon as possible. Get things taken care of while you have access to your spouse's income: car repairs, updated wardrobe, medical issues, and so on. Most importantly, it's time to find a job. You may end up with a substantial part of your spouse's assets, alimony payments, and child support that will help you once the divorce is final, but in the meantime, you may be cut off from access to any of this and may need to support yourself.

Q: Should one of us move out of our house?

A: This is a very tricky question to answer. First, if you or your children are in danger or if your spouse has a history of abuse, ensuring the safety of yourself and your children is always the number-one priority. If you can't move out, you can go to court for a protective order and ask a judge to order your spouse to leave. If you can take your children and leave, you will need to get a court order for temporary custody so your spouse cannot accuse you of kidnapping the children.

If there is no violence in your home, it can still be a miserable situation to continue to live with your spouse after you have agreed to divorce. Some couples continue to do so because they

can't make their income stretch to cover the cost of two living situations—especially when there are children involved, as you will
want to provide another home for them that maintains a decent
standard of living.[8]

If you are the higher-earning spouse, you will be expected
to continue to pay a larger share of the mortgage and household
expenses, as well as provide child support if your spouse remains
in the family home. This means that if you move out, your new
living situation will most likely be less desirable than you might
prefer. The spouse who stays in the home after the divorce is finalized may ultimately receive less money from the final divorce
settlement, because that spouse got the house.

In most states, divorce laws require that all property owned
during the marriage be divided equitably, which can mean that you
and your ex-spouse will have to sell the family house and divide the
money. In such a situation, you do not lose your claim to the house
because you are the spouse who moved out of it. If you continue
to make your share of the mortgage payments, insurance, and
upkeep, you have as much claim to the house as your spouse, who
continues to live in it.[9]

Some states will take adultery, abandonment, desertion, and
abuse into account when dividing property in a divorce. If this is
the case in your state and you are guilty of any of these charges,
you can expect to lose more of the property you shared with
your spouse.

....

8. Susan Bishop, "Should You Move Out of the Family Home during a Divorce?,"
DivorceNet.com, accessed January 8, 2014, http://www.divorcenet.com/resources
/divorce/marital-property-division/should-you-move-out-family-hom.

9. "Comparing Equitable Distribution and Community Property for a Divorce,"
LegalZoom.com, accessed January 8, 2014, http://www.legalzoom.com/divorce-guide
/equitable-distribution-community-property.html.

CHAPTER TWO

Understanding Divorce Laws

It's never advisable to leave "all that legal stuff" to your attorney, because no one will ever represent your own best interests as well as you can. You need to be aware of what's happening every step of the way to be sure that you've received your fair share of the marital property, and to be sure that you have not agreed to terms that are not beneficial to you once the divorce becomes final. The more you know before you begin the process, the less stress you will feel as the paperwork and procedures mount up around you. If you take the time to educate yourself now about the various aspects of divorce law, you will be able to both anticipate your attorney's needs and be a more effective participant in your own proceedings.

Divorce and the Law: The Basics

The most important thing to understand from the outset is that every state's divorce laws are different. While the end result is the same—your marriage comes to a legal end—the reasons you can give for wanting a divorce vary widely depending on your state's statutes. Issues of child custody, child support, spousal support, and property division can be different from state to state as well. If this is your first experience with your state's legal system, you will need to learn some new vocabulary and understand the way the courts handle divorce.

The most basic term in that new vocabulary is *residency require-ment,* and it may surprise you to learn that your state requires you to file for divorce in the county in which you live, not in the one where you got married (unless, of course, those two are the same). Most states require you to live in a county or parish for a specific amount of time before you can file for divorce. If you have just moved into a new area, you may need to file in the county where you previously lived. Your attorney, mediator, or the website for the county where you live will provide the information you need about residency requirements.

Once you know where you will file, you need to determine the *grounds* for your divorce. Your grounds are the legally acceptable reasons that you want the marriage to end. Acceptable grounds can vary widely from state to state and may include some or all of the following:[1]

- **Cruel and inhuman treatment:** Physical, verbal, psychological, and/or sexual abuse, that makes your continued living together unsafe for you and/or your children.

- **Abandonment:** One of you has left the other for a continuous period defined by the state (usually a year or more) without cause—such as escaping abuse—or without the other spouse's consent.

- **Constructive abandonment:** Takes place when one spouse has refused to have sex with the other for a period of at least one year, without the other spouse's consent.

- **Prison term:** If one of the spouses has been incarcerated for a crime for a number of years determined by the state.

- **Adultery:** Any sexual act with a person other than the spouse during the period of the marriage.

....

1. "Fault vs. No-Fault Divorce," NationalParalegal.edu, accessed January 8, 2014, http://nationalparalegal.edu/public_documents/courseware_asp_files /domesticRelations/Divorce/FaultVsNoFaultDivorce.asp.

- **Separation:** A period of living apart in anticipation of a permanent split, through a legal agreement or otherwise (depending on the state's laws).

- **Irreconcilable differences:** Sometimes referred to as an "irretrievable breakdown" in the relationship, in which the two spouses can no longer tolerate living together and the relationship cannot be repaired. States that consider this situation grounds for divorce usually set a minimum time in which these differences have made the living situation unbearable, such as six months to a year.

- **No-fault divorce:** Neither party needs to prove that the other has done anything wrong. In a no-fault divorce, which most states permit, a spouse cannot threaten to contest the proceeding, so there is no ugly courtroom battle—although the fight over division of property may still be contentious.

If you are the party filing for divorce, you will need to know the grounds that will be legally acceptable to the court in your state. You also will need to prove these grounds, showing that your complaint against your spouse can be justified with legal fact. Proof most often comes into play when your complaint against your spouse is adultery. Gathering evidence of this can be tricky, even with all the technology available: e-mail accounts, mobile phone logs, phone bills that list every call, and bank and credit card statements that track travel expenditures. Before you begin downloading and copying records in your spouse's name, consult your attorney to be sure that you come upon this information legally. Use of your spouse's confidential passwords without his or her consent can be considered felony computer misuse in some cases.

Next, determine if your divorce will be *contested* or *uncontested* (more detail on this distinction to come later in the chapter).

- An **uncontested** divorce means that you and your spouse have reached an agreement about your desire to end the marriage and about the division of your property and assets. You agree on child custody and support as well as spousal support. If you can work out all these issues before you file for divorce, the process will go swiftly.

- A **contested** divorce is one in which you and your spouse have not come to agreement on one or more issues. Perhaps one of you does not want a divorce, or you disagree about the grounds, the division of property, or custody of the children.

Once you have determined your residency, the grounds for your divorce, and whether your divorce will be contested or uncontested, you can begin to assemble the many documents you will need to proceed. You can download forms and other documents from your state's divorce website, or you can work with your attorney.

Your divorce process officially begins with a *petition*—a document filled out and written by one spouse and served to the other. If you write the document, you become the petitioner; if your spouse writes it, then your spouse is the petitioner. The spouse who receives the petition is called the *respondent.*

The petitioner delivers the petition to the respondent by way of any person over eighteen years old, which can be you if your divorce is amicable and you feel safe delivering the papers personally. You don't need to hire a professional *process server* unless your spouse deliberately tries to dodge receiving the petition or refuses to sign the papers. The respondent can then provide a response to the petition if he or she chooses. A response that shows agreement can help your divorce move along more quickly, most likely allowing you to avoid a court hearing. If the respondent disagrees with the petition and provides a response saying so, you can expect a lengthier process.

Once the receiving spouse signs the petition, your waiting period begins, and many things fall into place at this point. If your state requires a separation before the divorce is finalized, it can begin when the petition is signed. In all cases, the filing of a signed petition means that you and your spouse cannot take your children out of state, sell any of your property, take out loans using the property as collateral (you cannot take a home-equity line of credit to help you pay for your divorce and living expenses), or sell any insurance that covers the other spouse.

In addition, the signed petition automatically triggers a *restraining order* for both you and your spouse, preventing either of you from using your assets—bank accounts, lines of credit, and so on—for anything except "reasonable living expenses." If either you or your spouse attempt to hide assets or take out large sums of money once the restraining order is in place, you can be held in contempt of a court order—a situation that can result in a hefty fine or other penalties. The judge may also see reason to take this attempt at subterfuge into account when deciding on your right to child custody or visitation hours.[2]

What this automatic restraining order does *not* do, however, is protect you or your spouse from bodily harm. If your marriage is ending because of domestic violence, the victim of this abuse needs to file for an *emergency protective order* (EPO) or a *temporary restraining order*, either of which will forbid the spouse from contacting the victim, entering or damaging the victim's property, or approaching the victim or the couple's children. The EPO usually only remains in effect for a few days, so once you have received the EPO, you can file for a permanent protective order.[3]

Much of the rest of the divorce process will hinge on the division of your marital property and the custody of your children. Essentially, you and your spouse have a great deal of room to negotiate through the issues of custody, support, and division of property and assets, as long as you both agree on the final decisions. The court (and your attorney, should you use one) will want to see that the agreements you make are fair to both parties, so that neither of you takes advantage of the other and neither has the opportunity to exact revenge by taking more than their fair and legal share.

....

2. Ken LaMance, "Automatic Restraining Order," LegalMatch.com, accessed January 9, 2014, http://www.legalmatch.com/law-library/article/automatic-restraining-order .html.

3. Ken LaMance, "Emergency Protective Orders," LegalMatch.com, accessed January 9, 2014, http://www.legalmatch.com/law-library/article/emergency-protective-orders .html.

Understanding Your State's Divorce Laws

The divorce laws in each state are there to help you through the process, creating a basic structure within which you, your spouse, and your attorneys will work to reach an equitable agreement that will end your marriage, divide your property, and provide for your children.

State divorce laws can vary widely, so it's important to understand what your specific state requires in terms of grounds, proof of grounds, forms and other paperwork, and the many other issues that can slow down the process if not followed to the letter. Every state has a website for its courts, and every one of these websites has a section that specifically deals with the requirements for divorce in that state. If you don't know where to look for this information, start at DivorceSupport .com, a site that provides links to every state's information on divorce law and requirements.

In addition to the residency requirement discussed earlier, most states also require a waiting period before your divorce is finalized. On average, the waiting period is six months, but it can be shorter or longer depending on where you live. It is unrealistic to expect to file for divorce and walk away a free person on the same day.

Besides waiting periods and residency requirements, another important issue to your case is whether your state follows *equitable distribution* laws or *community property* laws.

- **Equitable distribution** means that the property you acquired during the marriage belongs to you, and the property your spouse acquired belongs to your spouse. As part of the divorce proceeding, the property will be divided in as equitable a manner as possible, providing each of you with relatively equal worth. This may mean that one of you gets the house and the other gets the equivalent value from your combined savings, for example. In general, a spouse receives between one-third and two-thirds of the marital property.

- **Community-property states** see the assets earned by the two spouses as owned by both of them. The states of Arizona, California, Idaho, Louisiana, Nevada, New Mexico, Texas,

Washington, and Wisconsin are all community-property states, so if you live in one of these, you and your spouse have claim to each other's earnings as well as all the property and savings acquired during the marriage. You can expect to divide everything accordingly—in half—which can mean the liquidation of property to split assets evenly. If you are the lower-earning spouse and you live in a community-property state, you may think this will work to your advantage—but you and your spouse also own all your debts equally, so you will carry half of the debt load when you leave the marriage, regardless of how that debt was accumulated.[4]

Divorce Alternatives

Under specific circumstances, you may be able to separate from your spouse via legal separation, civil annulment, or religious annulment.

Legal Separation

A legal separation is an option for people who are hoping that their marriage may be salvageable, but who need time apart to assess the situation. This agreement requires all the negotiation, division of property, and child custody decisions of a divorce, but you and your spouse remain married and live apart. A court order outlines the obligations and rights that both you and your spouse have within the relationship. This arrangement protects your interests while you and your spouse live separately, until you decide whether you want to continue your marriage or end it with a divorce. Because you are still married, a legal separation allows both spouses to continue to share the same medical insurance and other benefits. It also allows you to remain married but live separately, respecting one or both spouses' religious beliefs if divorce runs counter to your faith.

....

4. "Comparing Equitable Distribution," LegalZoom.

If you do decide to divorce after a period of time, your state may permit a *conversion divorce*, which simply converts your legal separation into a full divorce. In this case, the judge may assume that you have already come to an equitable agreement concerning your finances and children, so you may not have an opportunity to renegotiate. Be sure that the separation agreement represents you and your best interests for the long term.

Civil Annulment

A civil annulment declares a marriage null and void as if it never took place. While each state has its own specific set of laws governing annulment, they tend to agree on the circumstances that might warrant one:

- **Force:** If either spouse was forced into the marriage

- **Incest:** If the spouses are closely related—that is, brother and sister or first first cousins—or in another relationship forbidden by state law

- **Bigamy:** If one spouse had been married before and the divorce was never finalized

- **Misrepresentation:** If a spouse has been married before and has never revealed this to the new spouse, or if one spouse does not reveal issues such as impotence, inability to have children, a sexually transmitted disease, or a criminal record

- **No consummation:** If one spouse did not reveal before marriage that he or she is physically unable to have sexual intercourse

- **Intoxication or unsound mind:** If one spouse was too drunk or on drugs at the time of the marriage, or if he or she was cognitively impaired to the point at which legal consent could not have been given

- **Age:** If one of the spouses is under the age of consent in the state in which the marriage took place

Civil annulments usually take place very shortly after the wedding day—within a few days, weeks, or months—so this marriage dissolution process may happen fairly quickly, without the burden of dividing marital property and providing a custody agreement for children. Even when misrepresentation or other issues come to light later in the marriage, most states have specific laws governing the division of property and child custody in such a situation.

Religious Annulment

The Catholic Church has its own process of religious annulment for its members who qualify. The church expects its members to marry for life, but it does have a separation process of its own that allows its members to remain in the church despite the fact that they are leaving a marriage. The church's examination of your marriage can be time consuming and painful, but for those who are devout, it's a necessary process if you wish to remarry within the church sometime in the future. The Catholic Church considers annulment for people in the following situations:

- **Diriment impediment:** If one of the spouses is impaired in a way that should have prevented the marriage from taking place, this obstacle is called a diriment impediment. Issues that are considered an impediment to marriage include:

    - being too young to marry (the church sets the limit at sixteen years old for boys and fourteen for girls)

    - psychological incapacity

    - homosexuality

    - intoxication or drug abuse

    - bigamy

    - an inability to perform sexually or an aversion to sex that was not revealed before the marriage

- impediment of crime—killing or having one's spouse killed so that the living spouse can remarry

- consanguinity—a close relationship by blood or law (for example, marrying your natural brother, your adopted brother, or your stepbrother)

- affinity—a close relationship by marriage (for example, a man marrying his wife's sister)

- absence of the intention to have children

- **Defect of consent:** One of the spouses did not have "sufficient use of reason" to be able to consent to the marriage:

  - Raptus—One party abducts the other with the intention of marrying him or her.

  - Pregnancy—The man marries the woman for the sole reason that she is pregnant and he feels it is the right thing to do.

  - One of the spouses wants to marry solely to escape an unhappy home life.

  - The parents have arranged the marriage without the consent of the children involved.

- **Lack of canonical form:** The marriage does not follow the tenets of the Catholic Church:

  - The marriage was not conducted in front of a priest and is therefore not recognized by Catholic law.

  - The male spouse is an ordained member of the Catholic clergy.

  - Either spouse made a vow of chastity in a religious order.

  - One party is Catholic, while the other is not (and no dispensation to marry out of the faith was obtained in advance).

If you are a member of the Catholic Church and you want to obtain an annulment of your marriage, consult your parish priest or your local diocese. The process can be expensive and lengthy, but it may be required if you hope to remarry in the eyes of the church one day.[5]

Types of Divorce

The discussion of contested versus uncontested divorce began earlier in this chapter. Here's a closer look at these and other types of divorces:

- You are in a **contested divorce** when you cannot agree on issues that you must settle before the divorce is final. You may disagree on child custody, the size of support payments, division of property, or issues that are very specific to your individual case. When you can't agree, you need a judge to hear the case and make the decision for you—which means you must involve your attorney and your spouse's attorney. This process is called litigation, which simply means that you will engage in legal proceedings to bring the disagreement to a conclusion.

  In a contested divorce, the judge takes control of the proceeding, and you must abide by his or her decision once you receive it. You have the option of an appeal, but this is a costly process that involves a number of court appearances before an appeals judge or judges, followed by a new court date to finalize the divorce agreement should your appeal be successful. If your appeal is denied, you have spent a lot of money for no gain—and you have delayed the finalizing of your divorce by months.

- An **uncontested divorce** takes place when you and your spouse come to an agreement about all the terms of your split—division of property, spousal and child support, and child custody—without a court date or a need to litigate. The vast majority of divorces take this route, often with the help of a mediator to sort out the specifics of division of property and other issues. (More

....

5. "Frequently Asked Questions about Reasons/Grounds for Obtaining a Marriage Annulment," CatholicDoors.com, last modified September 3, 2011, http://www .catholicdoors.com/faq/qu79.htm.

on mediated divorce in this section.) To be sure that the uncontested divorce is fair to both parties, the spouses present their agreement to the court for approval, and the finalization of the agreement takes place more quickly than if the parties involved decide to litigate. Equally important is the fact that the cost of an uncontested divorce can be quite low, especially if no attorneys are involved. Most states charge less than $350 for a basic filing of an uncontested agreement.

- **At-fault divorce** takes place when one of the spouses has done something that makes the marriage intolerable to the other. Infidelity, physical or psychological abuse, desertion, alcohol or drug addiction, gambling addiction, or commission of a crime can all be causes of at-fault divorce. The spouse petitioning for the divorce bears the burden of proof, and he or she must be able to produce sound evidence that the other spouse has committed the act in question. This kind of divorce proceeding is less necessary than it once was, because a no-fault divorce is legal in all fifty states.

- **No-fault divorce** does not require proof that one spouse is at fault, allowing the spouses to end their marriage simply by citing "irreconcilable differences" or "irretrievable breakdown," depending on the law in the state of residence. Either spouse can apply for the divorce based on these grounds, even if the other spouse disagrees that the marriage has reached this point. The fault of either party will not be taken into consideration to end the marriage and finalize the divorce.

  That being said, the court may still consider the fault of one spouse or the other in determining the division of assets and debts, and in examining the options for child custody and visitation. Going with a no-fault divorce does not mean, for example, that equal custody will be granted to a spouse who has been habitually abusive, has endangered children, or who has an alcohol or drug dependency.

- A court can grant a **default divorce** if your spouse cannot be found or fails to respond to your petition.

- A **summary divorce** or **simple divorce** can be granted in some jurisdictions when the marriage lasted for fewer than five years, there are no children, the couple does not own a house or any other real property, and each spouse's personal property is worth less than a threshold set by the state (usually around $35,000). With nothing to split between them and no child custody agreement to reach, the marriage can end simply and quietly. If your marriage fits this description, check with your state to see if this option is open to you.

- **Mediated divorce** involves a professional mediator—a neutral third party—who is trained to assist with communication and negotiation between the two spouses. A mediator can help you resolve issues without the contentious proceedings often involved in a divorce that goes to court. Attorneys are not involved in the process, so the cost can be much lower for both of you.

- **Arbitration** is different from mediation in that it involves a private judge who acts as the arbitrator. You must agree to honor the decision of the arbitrator before the process begins.

- **Collaborative divorce** involves attorneys who work cooperatively to settle your case. You and your spouse each have your own attorney, but they are trained to work together to create the most equitable agreement possible. The collaboration requires you to disclose all the information necessary for negotiations, and to meet and work together, along with your attorneys, to discuss the settlement. If the collaboration breaks down and you need to proceed to court, the attorneys who worked on the collaborative divorce with you will withdraw, and you and your spouse will need to hire new attorneys to take the case to the next step.

Same-sex couples can now marry in seventeen states, so if you are gay or lesbian and your marriage comes to an end, you will be required to go through a divorce proceeding. The same is true for same-sex couples who have registered as domestic partners or who have married under a state's civil union law: Should you decide to end your relationship, you also must be legally divorced.

The type of divorce you eventually use will be based on your continued relationship with your spouse—whether the two of you can carry on an amicable and constructive dialogue, or if there is too much animosity between you to do so. An effort to work cooperatively can save both of you the cost of multiple attorneys and court hearings while bringing your marriage to a swift, fair, and comparatively painless end.

Resources for Understanding Divorce Laws

- **AllLaw.com:** This law portal has information on many issues, including divorce, family law, and child custody.

- **Cornell University Law School Legal Information Institute (www.law.cornell.edu/wex/divorce):** This venerable law school's website provides consumer-level information on various legal matters.

- **DivorceOnline.com:** Navigate to www.divorceonline.com/state -divorce-laws/ and click on the link for your state to find detailed pages on your local divorce laws.

- **DivorceResourceCenter.com:** This site provides articles, links, and personal stories for people facing an unwanted divorce.

- **FindLaw.com:** The dictionary page on this website (dictionary .findlaw.com/legal-glossary/divorce-and-family-law.html) provides quick definitions to many of the terms you will hear used by your attorney or the court system.

- **LawyerLocator.com:** This site provides basic information on divorce law and a search function to help you find a divorce attorney in your community.

- **MyDivorcePapers.com:** A series of videos on this site can help you understand how the law will affect specific issues, including distribution of retirement-plan funds, debt, real estate, other property, child support, and many others.

- **Nolo.com:** Go here for one of the web's largest libraries of legal information for consumers.

- **Pace University Law School Women's Justice Center (www .law.pace.edu/divorce-q):** This site provides a detailed question-and-answer page on divorce, with links to the responses that are of greatest interest to you.

CHAPTER THREE

Know Your Rights

Every person in America has the same legal rights granted to him or her by the United States Constitution. In the eyes of the law, you and your spouse have equal rights to make decisions in the best interests of your children, to live in the home you both share, to use joint funds and credit cards, and to sell, give away, or dispose of your property. These rights can be overridden by a court order, if necessary, to protect one spouse and the children. Once you file for divorce, however, your rights depend on the state in which you live. It's imperative that you understand your state's specific divorce laws so that you can protect your own interests as the case goes forward.

How to Begin to Understand Your Legal Rights

Every state has information available to help you understand its divorce laws, whether or not you are working with an attorney. Begin with a search on your state government's website to determine what laws and regulations are in place to protect your rights throughout the proceeding. Your rights will fall into a number of categories:

- **Protection:** If your spouse is abusive or you have reason to fear for the safety of your children or yourself, you have a right to legal protection. This is true in every state.[1]

....

1. "US State and Territorial Coalitions," NNEDV.org, accessed February 3, 2014, http://nnedv.org/resources/coalitions.html.

- **Alimony (spousal support):** The lower-earning spouse may or may not have a right to support from the higher-earning spouse. Even if you have been a homemaker for the duration of your marriage and you must continue to stay home with young children, you may be eligible only for limited support under the alimony-reform laws in some states.

- **Child support:** Many states have worksheets to determine appropriate child support, based on the income of both spouses. The spouse who has primary custody of the children does not always have the right to financial support from the other spouse. In the end, the right to financial support may actually belong to the child, not the parents—a safeguard put in place to keep parents from deciding independently that no child support will be paid.

- **Child custody:** Laws regarding custody vary significantly from one state to another, but all of them put the best interests of the child above all other considerations. While many couples approach a custody discussion with the assumption that the mother has the first right to primary custody, this is not the case in many states. You may find that your state presumes that parents will share joint custody, giving each parent relatively equal time with the child—unless the child's safety is in any way jeopardized. An abusive parent has very few rights in any state when it comes to child custody.

- **Property:** You may expect to walk away with the heirloom furniture you brought into the marriage, but state laws concerning property can vary widely. The state may legislate that you have the right to keep any property you owned before you were married, or those belongings may be considered part of the community property you now share as a married person.

- **Savings and investments:** Just as all your belongings may be considered community property in your state, things like your monetary inheritance from your Aunt Sarah may also be up for division. Your right to keep the savings you acquired before or during the marriage—including your 401(k) from your employer, the income from a business you own, or the individual retirement account (IRA) you have been funding every year—will be decided by your state's laws.

- **Debts:** State law will determine whether you have a right to walk away from debts incurred by you and/or your spouse for purchases, household expenses, college tuition, or any other means. You may find that your state expects you to continue to make mortgage payments even though you no longer live in the family house, especially if your children continue to live there. A debt load may be split between the two spouses or shifted to one spouse—whatever the judge determines is the most equitable arrangement.

- **Residence:** While it is common for the parent who has primary custody of the children to continue to live in the family home, this is not his or her legal right; it's part of a settlement agreement between both spouses. Do not assume that you have a right to stay in the house, or that the other spouse will be obligated by the court to make mortgage payments on the house.

How to Protect Your Legal Rights

Amid the shock, upset of your home life, and initial friction that comes with the decision to divorce, it can be all too easy to get bound up in emotion, preventing you from thinking clearly and taking quick action. If you are the surprised spouse and your husband or wife comes to you with a preliminary agreement that will "make everything easier," you may find yourself caught in a web of legal issues that will be bad for you later in the process.

Whether you are the spouse who files for divorce or the one who might not have seen it coming, your first steps must be to protect your own interests. You may need to maintain the status quo as best you can while you sort out your next move. Here are just a few important tips for what to do during this uncertain period:

- **Don't sign anything right away.** If you are the recipient of the news that your marriage is over, your spouse may have prepared an agreement about the division of your property, or he or she may bring you the divorce petition to sign. This is not the time to be passive and cooperative. You need time to review the paperwork and enlist the assistance of an attorney if you so choose.

- **Don't move out immediately.** This is most critical when you have children living at home. Moving out and leaving the children with your spouse may mean that you will have a tougher custody battle later. On the other hand, moving out and taking the children can give your spouse the impetus to have you arrested for kidnapping. If it's at all feasible, stay in the home and find ways to interact with your spouse as little as possible. Some couples find a time-sharing arrangement more tolerable: One spouse stays in the home while the other stays elsewhere, switching every few days.

- **Seek legal counsel.** This doesn't necessarily mean that you hire an attorney immediately, but you will be well served by paying an attorney for an initial consultation to be sure you don't make any missteps from the outset.

- **Make copies of important papers.** You can get bank statements, credit card statements, investment records, and other papers online if you have the passwords to these accounts. Make copies of anything you can't retrieve online: your mortgage, car loan statements, stock certificates, and so on.

- **Take inventory.** You and your spouse probably have accumulated a houseful of property, even if you've been married only a few years. You don't need to write down every teaspoon, but an itemized inventory of large items and categories of smaller ones will help you be sure that you've divided things equitably down the line. Use a spreadsheet program like Google Docs or Microsoft Excel and note the value of the large items as well as where and how you came to have them (joint purchase, came with one of you when you joined households, inherited, and so on). This will factor into who ends up with what.

- **Cancel your joint credit cards.** If your spouse has not already done so, spend a few minutes on the phone and cancel joint cards to keep anyone from making big purchases or taking large cash advances. At this stage, there's no telling who will end up with which debts, and you don't want to start your new life with a carelessly acquired debt load.

- **Store your valuables off-site.** If you have your mother's diamond earrings, an antique tea set that belonged to your great-aunt, a potentially valuable coin collection, or other items that could fetch a tidy sum if sold, now is the time to find a new, safe place for them.

- **Be an angel.** Do not give your spouse anything he or she can use against you to limit your visitation or your right to custody of your children. This is not the time to begin an affair, stay out all night, take up drinking, rack up moving violations, or commit any act of violence.

- **Protect yourself and your children.** If your spouse becomes violent toward you or the children, call the police. The report you file will come to the court's notice when it's time to discuss custody. If the violence happens again, seek a restraining order, or make plans to get out of the house with the children. The National Domestic Violence Hotline at 1-800-799-SAFE can help by connecting you with the resources you need in your area.

Do You Need an Attorney?

With divorces happening in more than 40 percent of all marriages in America, odds are you know someone who has been through a messy divorce—and you may know other people who managed to pull through without much animosity or difficulty. The kind of divorce you have depends in part on the people you and your spouse are, and what issues have driven you to seek a legal end to your marriage.

You can take some control over the tone of your divorce proceedings through the type of assistance you choose to engage. You have several options:

- **A professional mediator:** You and your spouse work with one person who represents both of you, and assists you in improving communication in order to reach a cordial understanding. A mediator is experienced in helping couples come to an equitable agreement about the division of their property, spousal support, child support, and child custody. This option removes the court from the process until you have an agreement in hand and can file an uncontested divorce petition.

- **A team of collaborative attorneys:** You and your spouse each select an attorney who takes a collaborative approach to the divorce settlement. You, your spouse, and your two attorneys come together to reach an agreement over all the issues of property and children, with each attorney working in his or her client's best interest, with the ultimate goal of coming to an equitable arrangement.[2]

- **A divorce attorney:** You and your spouse each hire an attorney whose goal it is to represent you and get everything they can from the other, working entirely for your benefit. You can choose from a wide range of divorce attorneys who have different styles: a litigator who will be eager to go to court and fight for your share of the settlement; a negotiator who will do his or her best to avoid a court battle by working toward a fair settlement; or one who is interested in helping you reach a friendly accord with your spouse.

- **Pro se:** If your divorce is uncontested and you and your spouse have no children and few assets, you have the option of representing yourself in your divorce proceedings. You will be responsible for filling out all the forms, filing everything on time with the

....

2. "Divorce: Do You Need a Lawyer?," Nolo.com, accessed January 9, 2014, http://www.nolo.com/legal-encyclopedia/divorce-do-you-need-lawyer-29502.html.

court system, and being fully prepared for any court appearances that take place. If you are in a contested divorce, however, self-representation should be the course of last resort. If you can't afford any kind of legal counsel, you may qualify for publicly funded legal aid and be matched with an attorney who can take your case at little or no cost.[3]

How do you decide which way to go? Take the following quiz. Your answers will help you determine the best course of action.

Quiz: Should You Get an Attorney?

For each "yes" answer, add two points to your score. For each "no" answer, add one point.

Do you and your spouse agree on the division of your financial assets?	Yes	No
Can you and your spouse agree on child custody and visitation?	Yes	No
Have you and your spouse agreed on what will be done with the family home?	Yes	No
Do you and your spouse agree about how your children will be raised—such issues as the school district they will attend, the religion in which they will be raised, and the value system you want to instill in them?	Yes	No

....

3. Cathy Meyer, "Pro Se Divorce Litigation, Obtaining a Divorce without an Attorney," About.com, Divorce Support, accessed January 9, 2014, http://divorcesupport.about .com/od/yourlegalrights/a/pro_se.htm.

If you have not reached agreement on any of the issues listed previously, do you feel confident that you and your spouse could work these out with the assistance of a mediator?	Yes	No
Do you believe that your spouse will proceed in an honest and fair manner?	Yes	No
Are you comfortable extending equal custody of your children to your spouse?	Yes	No
Do you feel able to put aside feelings of anger and resentment toward your spouse?	Yes	No
Do you have copies of all your financial records, and those of your spouse?	Yes	No
Is your spouse cooperating with your requests for financial disclosure?	Yes	No
Do you feel that your children are safe with your spouse?	Yes	No
Has your spouse already hired an attorney?	Yes	No
Has your spouse demonstrated a willingness to settle your divorce amicably?	Yes	No
Are you willing to move calmly toward a fair settlement?	Yes	No

14–19 points: You have some issues to sort out—some of them large—and you may be looking at a contentious divorce with the potential for some fairly major battles. You probably will be best served by hiring an attorney, especially if your spouse has already done so.

20–24 points: Your divorce proceeding could go smoothly with a mediator or collaborative process, but you may want to research divorce attorneys in your area just in case mediation does not proceed well.

25–28 points: Chances are good that you could resolve your differences and come to an equitable settlement by using a mediator.

What to Look for in a Divorce Attorney

If it looks as if you will need an attorney for your divorce, here are some things to keep in mind (also see the checklist at the end of this chapter).

- **Experience:** Find an attorney who has handled a lot of divorce cases in your county. Your attorney should be familiar with the judges in your area and the kinds of decisions they have made for similar cases in the past.

- **Goals:** Find an attorney whose goals match yours. It's the attorney's job to fight for your best interests, but whether that fight will take the form of a negotiation or a bloody court battle is very much up to you and your spouse.

- **References:** If you have friends who have been through divorces, find out which attorneys they used and what they thought of the experience. If you don't know someone who has worked with an attorney you're considering, ask the attorney for a list of references. This should be a standard request that a law firm receives often, so if the attorney hedges on this, you may want to move on.

- **Cost:** Before you meet with the attorney for the first time, ask what this initial meeting will cost. Some attorneys will have the **first meeting** with you free of charge, while others will charge their standard hourly fee—and it should be worth it to you to pay the fee for the opportunity to decide on whether this attorney is right for you. Once you're in the meeting, be sure to ask about the attorney's **hourly rate** and what divorces similar to yours have cost the clients. Your attorney will require a **retainer**, which is essentially a down payment on the services the firm will provide; find out what the figure is before you make a decision. Ask what **additional costs** will be involved beyond the attorney's fees: accountants, court costs, deposition reporters, and other services that may be required.

- **Access:** When you talk to the attorney's references, ask them about their ability to reach the attorney, and how quickly he or she returns calls. There's nothing more frustrating than being in the middle of a legal battle and finding out that your representative in the fight can't be reached for days at a time.

- **Chemistry:** Your attorney needs to be a good match for your own personality and comfort level, especially if you're going to work together for a long time. If you doubt an attorney's competence or you lack confidence in his or her ability to represent you, there's no reason to hire that attorney. Most communities have a number of attorneys, so keep looking.[4]

Beyond finding a good match with an individual attorney, it's important to ask yourself what you want your attorney to do. Perhaps you'd like your attorney to handle the paperwork and make sure that everything is done properly and according to legal requirements, but you would prefer to handle the negotiations with your spouse yourself. If your spouse is amenable to this as well, you can work out the details and use your attorney as a sounding board as the process moves forward.

It's more likely, though, that you're looking for an attorney who will work passionately for your best interests—one who will sort out

....

4. "Preparing Your Divorce Lawyer Checklist," DivorceSupport.com, accessed January 9, 2014, http://www.divorcesupport.com/divorce/Preparing-Your-Divorce -Lawyer-Checklist-2944.html.

the knotty problems that need to be resolved so that you can end your marriage. The more honest you can be with yourself about what you want from your divorce proceedings, the more likely you are to find the right attorney to represent you.

Not many couples actively seek retribution on a grand scale when they begin their divorce. As the process moves forward, however, emotion can take over until they find themselves in the midst of a bitter courtroom battle involving their entire families—including their children. Some attorneys have an aggressive style that will lead to this kind of drama, while others are more likely to work with you to avoid the theatrics as best they can. Do your homework before you hire the attorney who will help you end your marriage: Talk to people who have worked with them, and get a sense of what you can expect.

In the end, even if you've been careful in your attorney selection and you've found the perfect match with your personality and goals, your spouse may have decided that today is a good day to get revenge for whatever issues drove you both to divorce. If this is the case, you may have no choice but to meet blow for blow and fight it out in court before a judge.

Litigation costs a lot more money than negotiation. Choosing an attorney who will fight like a bulldog in court may net you a larger share of the settlement, but it will absolutely cost you more money than mediation or another collaborative process. Even if you do end up with a larger share of the settlement, whatever you may gain may disappear when you write that last check to your bulldog attorney. If you can make the decision early on that you do not want your savings to drain away in settlement costs, you may save yourself, your spouse, and your family a great deal of pain and aggravation.

Finally, if you have children, think about how they will view your courtroom drama. Divorce cases that go to court take longer to settle, cause greater animosity between spouses, and often place the children in the middle of a tug-of-war between their parents. Your division will be difficult for them on its own, even if it happens in a very friendly way. Before you hire an attorney to ramp up the aggression, consider the impact of this decision on others.

There is much to consider when it comes to hiring an attorney. Use the following checklists to help you make sure you have all your bases covered.

Checklist for Your Attorney

✓ **Experience:** How many complex divorce cases has he or she handled?

✓ **Focus on divorce law:** Is this a divorce attorney, or a generalist who has handled a few divorces, or a collections specialist? You need a skilled divorce attorney.

✓ **Familiar with the most current divorce laws:** This comes with experience and a practice focused on divorce.

✓ **Availability:** Will this attorney return calls within twenty-four hours?

✓ **Confidence:** Do you believe this attorney can handle your case and stand up to a contentious divorce proceeding? Will he or she do what is necessary to protect your interests?

✓ **Gender (your preference):** Do you want to work with an attorney who is the same gender as you?

✓ **Personality traits you prefer:** Do you want an attorney who is intimidating? Aggressive? Assertive without aggression? Calm and collected?

✓ **Your specific questions:** What details of your case make your situation unique? Can this attorney handle your issues?

Checklist for the Attorney's References

✓ **Work ethic:** Was this a hardworking attorney? Was he or she up to the challenge of your complex case, and did he or she work to bring it to a swift conclusion?

✓ **Assertiveness:** Does this attorney take the initiative to move ahead? Did he or she deal effectively with the obstacles encountered from your spouse's team?

✓ **Comfortable relationship:** Is this attorney easy to work with? Were there any unexpected bumps in the road?

✓ **Supportive:** Is this an attorney who will listen to my views on what is happening during the case? Will he or she understand my emotions regarding this divorce?

✓ **Effective:** In the end, what did this attorney accomplish for you?[5]

....

5. Some of these items are from "Picking a Divorce Lawyer," DivorceSupport.com, accessed January 9, 2014, http://www.divorcesupport.com/divorce/Picking-a-Divorce-Lawyer-2942.html.

CHAPTER FOUR

Divorce and Finances

How much do you know about the financial condition of your marriage? You may be the spouse who handles all the finances and knows exactly where every penny resides. Or you may be entirely ignorant of your family's income and savings. Many people are somewhere in between. One of the largest mistakes a divorcing spouse can make is to be ignorant when it comes to finances. If you have always let your spouse take care of the bills, odds are he or she will be in a better position to negotiate when it comes to settling finances.[1]

If you don't handle the family finances, you will need to gather all the information you can as quickly as possible. While your attorney can demand that your spouse hand over the information you need to work through a settlement agreement, this is often a contentious and potentially costly process. The more you can put together on your own, the better idea you will have of what resources are available and what property and funds you may have coming to you in a settlement.

Understanding Your Property Rights

Property, in the legal sense, includes just about anything you and your spouse owned before or during your marriage. Your house, cars, home furnishings, clothing, jewelry, sports equipment, computers and other

....

1. Lina Guillen, "15 Critical Mistakes in Divorce," DivorceNet.com, accessed January 14, 2014, http://www.divorcenet.com/states/new_york/15_critical_mistakes_in_divorce.

office equipment, boat, real estate beyond your home, and any other physical things are property. So are your bank accounts, credit cards, investments, retirement accounts, and any other monetary accounts you may have. Intangible things can be considered property as well. If you own a patent on an invention, a trademark or service mark on a logo or business name, a copyright and royalty agreement on a book or music, or a professional license, all these things will count as property in a divorce proceeding. Your debts are considered property, too, because they are items that must be allocated to one spouse or the other. Debt will be subtracted from the value of the other property in determining the value of the final settlement.

In just about every state, the question of property ownership hinges on the *date of separation* (DOS)—the moment in time at which you and your spouse officially enter a holding period. States differ in what constitutes the actual DOS: In some states, the separation period begins when the divorce papers are filed, while others pinpoint the day on which you and your spouse stopped living in the same home. A few states consider the DOS to be the day that one spouse informed the other that he or she intended to file for divorce. As DOS can be a subjective date in instances like these, you may find yourself in a battle just to determine when your separation actually began—especially if there are major amounts of assets or debts at stake. The DOS becomes critically important when one spouse or the other uses the period before the DOS to run up lots of new debts, use joint credit cards, or drain savings accounts.

The sooner you can establish an official DOS, the more you will be able to shield yourself from unexpected debt or the sudden disappearance of savings and cash. At the same time, if you are due to receive a large sum from a retirement plan, an employee bonus, or another windfall, you may want to push for a DOS before such a payment arrives.

Once you have established the DOS and you are officially separated, you both still have obligations to make payments on debts, including the mortgage—even if you are not the one living in the house. You also have the right to use savings in joint accounts, with the understanding that you will take no more than half of what is available in any savings accounts, certificates of deposit, money market accounts, stocks, and so on, and that you use only what is available in accounts that are in both of your names or in your name only.

What your rights are in terms of the rest of the property depends on your state's laws, and whether they call for equitable distribution or community property (see chapter 2). In all cases, you have the right to your fair share of the property you and your spouse acquired during the marriage. You also have the right to property you acquired before the marriage, including gifts, inheritance, and your pension. If anything you brought into the marriage was somehow enhanced while you were married, however—for example, if you owned a business before you were married, and you and your spouse ran it together and doubled its size—then it most likely will be considered marital property by the court.

Access to your marital home is shared until your divorce is final, unless there is a temporary or permanent restraining order that says otherwise. Likewise, if you are the spouse who continues to live in the home through the divorce negotiations, you do not have the right to lock your spouse out of the house unless you have a court order allowing you to do so.[2]

Your Property versus Marital Property

Your property is anything that you acquired before the marriage and anything that you purchased with money you had before you were married. For example, if you received a substantial inheritance before you were married and you bought a Porsche convertible solely with that money, your convertible remains your separate property. If, however, you bought your Porsche partly with your inheritance money and partly with a home-equity line of credit on your house, a court will most likely decide that this car is marital property.

In general, marital property is anything you and your spouse acquired while you were married—from the living room sofa to the forks in your kitchen drawer. Anything earned during the marriage is considered marital property, too, so your income and your spouse's

2. "Divorce and Property," FindLaw.com, accessed January 10, 2014, http://family.findlaw.com/divorce/divorce-property.html?DCMP=GOO-FAM_Divorce -Property&HBX_PK=divorce+property+rights.

income, as well as your pension funds, savings accounts, retirement accounts, investments, and any other assets that arrived during the marriage, are all marital property and will be divided between you. The exception is an inheritance that was left specifically to one spouse or the other—this is considered personal (separate) property.

You may be tempted to try to hide assets from your spouse—particularly if you have been doing this for some time during your marriage—but this is a crime, and it's probably foolhardy to believe that your spouse does not know that this is happening. If your spouse has an inkling that there may be additional assets hidden somewhere, his or her attorney will certainly hire forensic accountants to find them. The discovery of hidden assets will not help your case.

Equitable Distribution of Property

If you live in a community-property state, you will be entitled to half of the total assets and debts acquired during your marriage. This does not mean that every asset must be liquidated; you, your spouse, and your attorneys or mediator will determine the total value of the assets and divide them into shares of equal value. In a community-property state, equal division also includes your income and that of your spouse—in other words, you are entitled to half of your spouse's income, and he or she is entitled to half of yours.

In an equitable-distribution state, the division of property is more complicated and takes many more factors into account. This list, compiled by certified divorce coach Cathy Meyer, will help you understand the kinds of information you will need to gather:

- the property each spouse brought to the marriage
- each spouse's income and earning potential
- the standard of living you and your spouse maintained during the marriage
- the length of the marriage

- each spouse's health—physical, mental, and emotional

- each spouse's standard of living and employment once the settlement goes into effect

- the contribution each spouse made to the other's education or training—that is, if you supported your spouse while he or she completed an advanced degree

- either spouse's contribution as a full-time caregiver to children or as a homemaker

- each spouse's contribution to making joint purchases of marital property

- the current value of anything you own together or separately

- the requirement for the primary parent to live in the home with the children, and the property and expenses required for this

- the outstanding debts incurred during the marriage

- any property you each owned before the marriage

- anything else that may be specifically relevant to your case

As you can see, the process for establishing a settlement can be complicated in a state with an equitable-distribution law. If it is at all possible for you and your spouse to decide on the division of property before meeting with your attorneys, it will save you some time and potential frustration later.

Protecting Your Assets

When you or your spouse file for divorce, an automatic restraining order goes into effect that prohibits either of you from selling, concealing, removing, or disposing of any property except as required for a "reasonable standard of living." You are both forbidden to incur any major debt from that point forward, or from changing the beneficiaries on your life insurance policies, pensions, or retirement funds. The order also prohibits you or your spouse from removing the other (or your children) from a family health insurance policy.

This all may seem harsh, but it's meant to be a safeguard against your spouse's selling or destroying anything you owned together, or draining your bank accounts and leaving you with no cash or available credit. It also protects your spouse from any action you might take in the same regard.

As discussed in "The First Ten Steps" in chapter 1, your best protection against shenanigans on your spouse's part is to collect all the financial information you can for all your accounts—in your own name and in both of your names. If you have access to them, collect and make copies of the statements for your spouse's accounts as well. (If you can't access these, your attorney can request this information—and use a subpoena if your spouse does not comply.) Use the checklist at the end of this chapter to gather all the information you can. This will give you a snapshot of your assets and debts at the time you filed for divorce. From that point forward, major changes in any of the accounts will raise red flags that your spouse is using assets and accumulating debts in ways that are not permitted by law.

Find all the purchase records for property you and your spouse bought during the marriage. If you paid for some of the items yourself with your own money, you may be able to lay claim to them as separate property; your spouse will be able to do so as well with any item he or she paid for with personal funds.

Records of your mortgage payments, capital improvements, and major repairs will reveal which of you has put more money into the family home. This can lead to a buyout situation where one of you keeps the home and pays the other spouse the amount he or she has put into the home. If you decide to sell the house and split the money, the spouse who has made more payments and paid the bills for home improvements may end up with a larger share of the purchase price.

If you happen to receive an inheritance just before the divorce process, don't put it into a joint account or add it to the family savings. If the bequest names only you as the beneficiary, this is considered separate property in an equitable-distribution state. You will not be required to split it with your spouse as long as you have not comingled it with joint savings. Still, in some states, if you use some of your inheritance money to make improvements to your family's home, this may change the money's status to a joint inheritance because both spouses and the family benefited from it. Talk with your attorney about the ways you have used your inheritance to understand how it may be viewed by the court.[3]

In the end, the most effective way to protect any property you brought into the marriage is with a prenuptial agreement signed by both spouses. If you had significant assets when you were single and you did not put together a "prenup" before you were married, you are no different from the vast majority of couples—but it will be more complicated to sort out your separate property from the marital property you shared with your spouse.

Protecting Your Credit

Joint credit card accounts seem like a wonderful convenience while you are married, but once you and your spouse decide to split, a joint account can be a nuisance that ties you to your spouse well beyond the date of divorce. In worst cases, a joint card can even become a tool in revenge. It is altogether too common that joint credit accounts go into arrears during a divorce proceeding, and that debts assigned to one spouse or the other are not paid in a timely manner. You need to take whatever steps you can to shield yourself from the possibility of default to be sure that your credit rating remains stable, and that you can get credit later when you need it.

First, look into closing joint credit card accounts. This is much easier said than done: To close the account, you will need to pay off the outstanding balance. When you are in the midst of a divorce, it can be the worst possible time for you to think about paying off a five-figure credit card debt—but it can also save you a great deal of aggravation down the road if you can manage to do it.

Your divorce decree may assign payment of the debt on the card to one spouse or the other. The credit card company was not part of that

....

3. "Inheritance and Divorce," FindLaw.com, accessed January 13, 2014, http://family .findlaw.com/divorce/inheritance-and-divorce.html.

contract, however, so it is under no obligation to observe that agreement. To the card issuer, you and your spouse are both named on the card, so you are equally responsible for 100 percent—not 50 percent each—of the debt. If payment of a joint credit card account is assigned to your spouse in the divorce decree and he or she defaults on the debt, it *will* show up on your credit report. You can take legal action (which will cost you more money) by petitioning the court to enforce the divorce decree. This will force your spouse to appear in court and explain why the debts are not being paid.[4]

At the same time, your spouse may go off on a revenge spending spree and run up a huge debt that you now have to pay off to save your credit rating. You have little recourse in such a case: The credit card company will not remove your name from the card, because the card was approved based on the strength of your and your spouse's combined income and credit. To remove your name, the company would have to review your spouse's credit and reassign the card to him or her—an option that requires your spouse's cooperation. If he or she is already dodging the obligation to make payments on this card, it's highly unlikely you will find much success by trying to take this route.

If you are lucky enough to be involved in a fairly amicable divorce, you may be able to negotiate an agreement with your spouse where you both pay off the balances on joint cards and close them together. In a perfect world, this would be the most reasonable solution, removing the potential that these joint cards will be used as weapons against each other down the road.

If you can't negotiate a reasonable deal with your spouse to eliminate the joint accounts early in the process, stipulate in your divorce decree that your spouse must notify you if he or she intends to miss a credit card payment. Make a point of checking your credit report on a monthly basis to catch any late payments or nonpayment activity. The sooner you take legal action to require your spouse to make the

. . . .

4. Janna Herron, "Close Credit Card Accounts in Divorce," Bankrate.com, accessed January 13, 2014, http://www.bankrate.com/finance/credit-cards/close-credit-card -accounts-divorce.aspx.

payments he or she agreed to make, the better you will be able to protect your own interests for the long term.[5]

In equitable-distribution states, if your spouse is the primary cardholder and you are an *authorized user* rather than a joint cardholder, you are not responsible for the debt unless you have agreed to pay part of it in the divorce settlement. The credit card company will not look to you for payments, and any missed payments will not show up on your credit report. This changes in community-property states, where all debts incurred during a marriage are considered joint debts. If you live in one of the nine community-property states (see chapter 2), your best course of action is to engage your spouse in an agreement to pay off the debt together and close the card.

Ten Ways to Find Hidden Assets

Divorce court makes the equal division of assets and debts a primary goal of the proceedings, so it's critical that you provide all the information you can to ensure that you get your fair share. It's equally important that you have all the real information you can get from your spouse.

Begin by making a list of all your personal assets, household assets, and all your debts—including your regular household expenses as well as your longer-term loans, credit card balances, mortgage, and any debts you may owe to specific people (such as your parents).

List all the assets your spouse has in his or her own name. Keep in mind that you may not know of every asset, especially if your spouse has been planning for this divorce longer than you have. It's possible that some property, cash, and income may be hidden from you—and possibly has been for quite some time. Your attorney will know of a number of ways that spouses disguise or hide assets from one another, so if you have any inkling that there may be things of value that have

....

5. "Getting Removed as Joint Credit Card Account Holder," Experian.com, accessed January 13, 2014, http://www.experian.com/blogs/ask-experian/2013/02/28/getting -removed-as-joint-credit-card-account-holder/.

not been disclosed, be sure to bring this up. Watch for any of the following signs that your spouse might be concealing assets from you:[6]

1. **Income versus lifestyle:** Your spouse reports rock-bottom income but suddenly has a number of expensive toys—and you're not seeing the charges for these on your credit card statements.

2. **Closed-mouthed about money:** Your spouse handles the financial matters for your family and suddenly won't share any information with you.

3. **Rocky self-employment:** Your spouse's business has always done well, and suddenly he or she reports that income has taken a nose-dive and costs are out of control.

4. **Surprise debts or gifts:** Your spouse decides to pay a friend or family member back for significant cash debts you've never heard mentioned before this. This is an almost sure sign that the family member or friend is going to hold this cash until your divorce is final, and then return it to your spouse.

5. **Pressure to sign:** Your spouse comes to you with documents to sign about financial transactions, wanting you to sign right away without spending time going over the document. These can turn out to be documents that remove your right to property or accounts.

6. **Sudden large withdrawals:** You find large cash withdrawals on bank statements for your checking or savings accounts, without any explanation from your spouse.

7. **Custodial accounts:** Your spouse sets aside a large sum of money in the name of one of your children, using the child's Social Security number, and establishes him or herself as the trustee for this account.

....

6. "Searching for Hidden Assets at Divorce," Nolo.com, accessed January 10, 2014, http://www.nolo.com/legal-encyclopedia/searching-hidden-assets-divorce-29968.html.

8. **Traveler's checks:** You discover wads of traveler's checks worth thousands of dollars, when neither you nor your spouse has special travel plans.

9. **Bonus delays:** Your spouse's boss inexplicably delays a major bonus or a raise, or your spouse reports that his employer is not giving bonuses this year when you know the business has done well.

10. **Suspicious charges:** You find charges to your spouse's credit card for gifts, hotel room nights, college tuition, rent, or travel, when none of this activity is for you or your family.

Your attorney may refer you to a forensic accountant or a private investigator, or he or she may recommend other formal discovery procedures that will help you determine if your spouse is dealing honestly with you.

Dividing Assets and Debts

Each state has its own laws for the division of assets and debts, but they all look to divide these items equitably between the two spouses. *Equitably,* however, does not necessarily mean *equally.* If there are reasons that one spouse should receive a larger share of the marital assets or debts, the court may decide to give more to this spouse.

You can divide assets by determining which items go to which spouse, working toward a fairly even distribution so that each of you ends up with roughly the same amount of value. This can mean that one spouse takes the family home, while the other spouse receives the equivalent value in investments, bank accounts, or other property. If there are not enough assets to allow one spouse to take the house and the other to take equivalent value, you may need to sell the house and divide the proceeds equally between you. Alternately, one spouse can buy out the other's share of the house.

If there is a business involved, your situation may become very complicated. Perhaps one spouse officially owns the business, but the other contributed a great deal to its success through his or her labor and expertise. You may both be entitled to a half share in the business, but extracting your half may cripple the business's ability to function. You and your spouse will need a skilled business attorney to set up a buyout figure that represents your contribution to the business, and a payment plan that will provide your fair share without crippling the enterprise.

If you have items that may have unusual value—antiques, artwork, heirlooms, jewelry, and the like—you will be best served by an independent appraisal of each of these items. Independent appraisal will keep one spouse from deliberately attempting to undervalue an item to make it less interesting to the other. The item's value then becomes part of the total assets to be divided.

As mentioned earlier, you and your spouse will also divide up the debts you have, and you will divide this debt as equitably as you divide assets. Your mortgage, credit card debt, home-equity lines of credit, money you borrowed against your life insurance, consumer and student loans, car loans, and any other debts that need to be repaid all get divided. Remember, credit card companies and banks do not recognize your separation agreement or divorce decree as binding documents for their purposes, so even if your spouse is assigned to pay off a joint credit card, you are still responsible for the debt if your spouse defaults.[7]

Understanding Alimony

Alimony—or spousal support, as the courts more commonly call it—is the amount of money one spouse pays another under a divorce decree. You (or your spouse) may qualify for spousal support under the laws of your state, based both on your need and your spouse's ability to pay. If one or more of the following scenarios applies to you, you should talk with your attorney or mediator about potentially receiving this kind of support from your spouse:

....

7. Ann MacDonald, "How Do Family Courts Split Up Debt upon Divorce?," LegalZoom.com, accessed January 13, 2014, http://www.legalzoom.com/marriage -divorce-family-law/divorce/how-do-family-courts-split.

- You're a full-time homemaker and at-home mother or father, and you have not worked outside the home for several years.

- You're a full-time homemaker and at-home mother or father, and you have never worked outside the home.

- You've been married more than ten years.

- You have been financially dependent on your spouse for many years.

- You supported your spouse financially while he or she earned a college degree.

- Your income is significantly lower than your spouse's income.

Do not assume that if you are a woman you will not have to pay alimony to your husband. If you have the larger income and he is an at-home father with full-time child-care responsibilities, it's very likely that you will pay spousal support to him when your divorce becomes final, even if he returns to the workforce right away.

Spousal support takes a number of different forms: permanent, temporary, or lump sum, each of which is required for a different purpose.

- **Permanent alimony** continues on a monthly basis until the recipient remarries or forms a long-term cohabitant relationship. This is only likely for full-time homemakers who have never held a job outside the home, and for spouses with disabilities or other reasons that they cannot earn their own income.

- **Temporary alimony** may be paid for a set period of months or years, after which the receiving spouse is expected to improve his or her own standard of living through personal income.

- **Lump-sum settlement** is an option instead of monthly payments when the spouse is in a position to pay a large sum at once, and comes with the advantage of severing the tie between spouses immediately rather than later. While the lump sum may be smaller than years of monthly payments, it may be useful if you are planning to make a down payment on a house, and you will not need to wonder every month if your spouse will make the alimony payment on time.[8]

In determining spousal-support payment, the court will take a number of factors into consideration, including:

- **Your standard of living during the marriage:** The court will try to help you and your spouse maintain that standard, though this may be difficult depending on the actual alimony payment you receive.

- **How long you were married:** If your marriage ended quickly and you have no children, the chances of you receiving alimony are very slim. A longer marriage, even without children, may net an alimony payment—especially if you were married for more than ten years.

- **Division of debt:** If you and your spouse accumulated a very large debt during your marriage, the spouse who ends up with the largest share of that debt probably will not pay alimony to the other. Relief from the debt by one spouse would be considered akin to spousal support.

- **Support through education:** If you worked to support your spouse while he or she finished graduate school and earned a professional degree, your chances of receiving spousal support improve in some states (especially if your spouse asked for a divorce shortly after graduating or completing the licensing program). Your support payments may continue for as many years as the degree program required, as compensation for your years of support.

- **Your age:** A judge will take your age and earning potential into consideration when determining if spousal support is warranted. If you are twenty-five and just beginning your career, you may not

....

8. "Divorce: Alimony Payments," WomensFinance.com, accessed January 13, 2014, http://www.womensfinance.com/wf/divorce/alimony1.asp.

get as much spousal support as you would if you were sixty and coming to the end of your working life.

- **Value of your assets:** If your settlement is substantial and you have a promising career, a judge may determine that you don't require alimony.[9]

Negotiating a Settlement Agreement

If at all possible, you and your spouse will be best served by negotiating a settlement before you file your petition for divorce, and before your official separation begins. This process can be fairly simple or very contentious, depending on the condition of your relationship as you begin. It's the most constructive path, however, as you will have much more opportunity to be heard in negotiations with your spouse and a mediator or with collaborative attorneys than you will in a court of law.

In most cases, a divorce settlement is not an opportunity to get rich. You do need to protect your own interests and those of your children, taking into account the resources that would have been available to you if you and your spouse remained married. During settlement negotiation, you will need to consider a number of factors to be sure your long-term financial needs and your children's education requirements will be funded by the settlement. These factors include:

- **Cost of living:** Put together a household budget to determine exactly how much money you spend every month, and on what. Your goal will be to maintain a reasonable standard of living after the divorce, so the more honest and forward thinking you are about the cash you need every month to live (taking into account a realistic expectation for inflation over the years), the more effective you can be in negotiating your settlement. Consider not only your own living expenses, but also those of your children.

....

9. Cathy Meyer, "How Do the Courts Determine Alimony?," About.com, Divorce Support, accessed January 13, 2014, http://divorcesupport.about.com/od /financialissues/f/alimonyconsider.htm.

For example, your child may play a sport that requires expenditures for equipment, uniforms, and trips to competitions. If you have an infant or toddler, day care is a legitimate expense that should be funded by both parents. These expenses may or may not be included in child support payments, depending on your state of residency, so make sure you include them in the settlement discussion.

- **Your house:** Depending on your situation, one spouse and the children may remain in the family home, or you may sell the home and split the money. If part of the family lives in the home, the nonresident spouse can expect to pay a portion of the living expenses, including utilities and repairs. If you are the custodial parent and the mortgage is too large for you to carry alone, selling the house may be the best option—giving you some cash to use to either rent or purchase a smaller house.

- **Health insurance:** If you have been covered on your spouse's health insurance policy, you will now have to purchase one of your own. Under the Affordable Care Act that went into effect on October 1, 2013, you may be able to buy a policy using discounts provided by the federal government, especially if your income is below a threshold established in each state. If your children have been covered on the other spouse's health insurance policy, there's no reason that they should not continue with that coverage.

- **College:** The more you can get on paper during your settlement process, the less likely it is that you will need to return to court in a decade or so to hash out issues with your spouse again. That's why there's no time like the present to determine who will pay how much for college tuition—even if your child is a baby. You don't need to insist that one of you cover all the costs of an Ivy League education, but you do need to establish a pattern of savings and an expectation of support once your child reaches high school graduation.

- **Retirement:** If you and your spouse have retirement accounts, you will need to split them between you, and this can be a worrying turn of events if you are close to retirement. If your savings are no longer enough to sustain you in a reasonable manner once you stop working, you and your attorney should discuss the options available to you as part of the settlement. Perhaps your higher-earning spouse can be required to contribute to your IRA, or you can negotiate for another asset you can sell when you need additional income.[10]

Financial Checklist

Much ground was covered in this chapter. As a way to help you prioritize and stay on track, here is a checklist of things you need to collect to gain a full understanding of your own (and your spouse's) financial situation.

✓ Personal income tax returns for the last three to five years

✓ Business income tax returns for the last three to five years

✓ Proof of your current income

✓ Proof of your spouse's current income

✓ Bank and investment statements: checking, savings, money market, CDs, financial adviser, and any others

✓ IRA, SEP, 401(k), and any other retirement-plan statements

✓ Pension statement, if you have one

✓ Life, health, homeowner's, and auto insurance policies

✓ Wills, trusts, and a living will

....

10. Cathy Meyer, "How to Negotiate the Best Possible Settlement," About.com, Divorce Support, accessed January 14, 2014, http://divorcesupport.about.com/od /propertydistribution/ht/divagreement.htm.

- ✓ Power of attorney
- ✓ Stock option statements
- ✓ Mortgage statements for all properties you and your spouse own
- ✓ Property tax statements
- ✓ Credit card statements
- ✓ Loan documents (car, home equity, consumer)
- ✓ Utility bills
- ✓ Other bills
- ✓ Appraisal documents on any valuable personal property or real estate
- ✓ Inventory of personal property, including photos of anything particularly valuable
- ✓ List of major property or valuables owned before you were married
- ✓ List of the contents of your safe-deposit box
- ✓ Copies of any other debts

PART TWO

Divorce and Children

CHAPTER FIVE

Emotional Well-Being

With all the emotional turmoil you feel about your divorce proceedings, it can be easy to forget—or simply to overlook—the impact the end of your marriage is having on your children.

Children see the world through the filter of their parents' words and actions, so they may be particularly confused by the behavior they see as you and your spouse split up to live separate lives. Despite your best efforts, they are likely to witness harsh words or fights between their parents—potentially showcasing a level of anger they may have never seen from you before. Confusion can give way to disillusionment and anger as they determine that you and your spouse have broken the trust that children have in their parents. Their perception of the situation can be colored further by fear, divided loyalties, guilt, and the sense that this upheaval of all your lives is somehow their fault.

While you can't avoid these feelings in your children, you can take steps throughout the process to recognize their fears, validate their emotions, and create an environment as emotionally safe as possible for your children to express their feelings.

Talking about the Decision

You may think it goes without saying that children should not find out about their parents' divorce by overhearing a shouting match—but all too often, that's how a child discovers that his parents are splitting up.

The worst part about this situation is that the parents may not even realize they have been overheard. With the information delivered accidentally, with tensions mounting in the household, and with clues piling up like so many packing boxes, the child often waits in fear for the parents to finally admit that they are divorcing. That day may take weeks or months to finally arrive.

By the time children are three or four years old, they can pick up quickly on clues that tell them that something is wrong in the family—and they understand far more than you may think. While they may not comprehend each and every detail of the conflicts between you, they certainly know that the both of you are mad all the time, and that one of you doesn't want to play with them after dinner anymore. As they get older, the cues that mean conflict become less and less opaque to them. The last thing you want to hear from your child when you tell him about your divorce is, "Well, it's about time you said something."

Once you and your spouse are sure that you are moving ahead with the divorce, plan a day and time to tell your children as soon as you can. You may dread the conversation and its impact on your children, but the sooner you do it, the sooner you can address your children's fears and make the entire situation less terrifying for them.

Discuss the conversation with your spouse ahead of time, and agree on the language you will use and the information you will share. Children of any age do not need to know every detail of your spouse's infidelity or whatever other breach may have contributed to the divorce, but they do need to understand that you have tried to reconcile your differences and have reached a final impasse.

Many parents become tongue tied or freeze up altogether when they have to talk about a subject their children will find painful. Your best defense against this is to know exactly what you want to say, and how you will say it. Ideally, you will rehearse this with your spouse—perhaps getting your anger and sarcasm out of the way before you sit down with your children. Ask each other the questions you think your children will ask you, and plan how you will answer them. You may not be able to anticipate every possible question, but knowing the language and tone you will use will help you respond to surprise questions with some confidence.

Above all, make a pact with your spouse that neither of you will turn this conversation with your children into an argument, even if your children lash out in anger. You will not gain your children's trust or quell their fears by having a family shouting match—in fact, that's exactly what they fear will happen. Keep your cool and avoid language that will cause tempers to flare.[1]

Here are some things to keep in mind as you plan the conversation:

- **Tell the truth, but don't blame your spouse.** You and your spouse are getting a divorce, and even a small child will not be fooled if you try to dismiss it as a minor occurrence or act as if nothing is really wrong. Your children want to know what happened between you, and they deserve a cogent explanation—but pointing fingers at one another will not help your child. Determine in advance what reason you will give, and gain your spouse's agreement on what you will say. "Mommy cheated on me," is probably not the best thing to say, but "We just can't get along anymore, so we've decided it's time to stop living together," is a fair statement.

- **Use an age-appropriate level of detail.** For example, a child in his late teens may be ready to hear that Mommy has determined that she is a lesbian, but a child who doesn't know what sex or romantic attraction are yet might not be ready for that level of detail. If you truly don't know what information your child can understand and cope with, consult a child counselor or social worker.

- **Explain what happens next.** You may not have all the details of your divorce settlement worked out, but your child does not need to know where every dollar will go. Your child's first concern will be where he will live, and with whom. If you plan to sell the house, your child has a right to know this. "We'll be moving to a new place in the same area" can be a comforting statement, as your child won't have to go to a new school district and make new

....

1. Gina Kemp, Melinda Smith, and Jeanne Segal, "Children and Divorce: Helping Kids Cope with Separation and Divorce," Helpguide.org, last modified December 2013, http://www.helpguide.org/mental/children_divorce.htm.

friends. "Daddy is moving to a new apartment, but you will see him for three days of every week" will help him understand that while the family relationship is changing, both parents will still be in the child's life. Tell him what will change, and emphasize the things that will not change—in particular, that you and your spouse will continue to love him, as you always have.

- **Be straightforward.** A discussion about a major life change is not the time for cute quips, personality jabs, rolling eyes, or sarcasm. Treat your child's reaction and emotions with respect, and with the same honesty that he is showing you.

- **Say, "We will always be here for you."** Younger children may decide that if people break up when they don't get along, then you might decide to break up with them when they're bad. This first realization that love can end may be a terrifying discovery to your young child, one that will make him fearful every time you raise your voice or seem irritated with him for years to come. Make it as clear as you can that parents never, ever divorce their children, and that you and your spouse will always love and protect him and want to be with him. This is a message you will need to reinforce through words and deeds for some time to come.

Understanding the Emotional Impact on Your Child

While you will certainly be preoccupied with the division of money and property and the whirlwind of emotion that comes with ending a marriage, your child can be equally preoccupied with your divorce—but from an entirely different perspective.

To your child, the normalcy of his home life has been shattered by divorce, and a new normal has been put into place without his involvement or approval. He sees less of either parent, and has to go someplace special—a new home or a temporary apartment—to see one of his parents. When he's with one parent, he hears comments about the other that he does not know how to process. Sometimes one parent might give him a message to tell the other, and the other might have an emotional reaction to the message, potentially leaving the child feeling guilty for delivering it. When his parents are both in the same place, they might bicker and snap at each other, making him feel anxious. If they argue about him, he might feel guilty. Over time, the child can turn some of this guilt into anger and resentment at one parent or the other—or sometimes both. Pulled between the two, and feeling as though he's supposed to be loyal to one parent and angry at the other, he may become withdrawn and uncomfortable with both of you.[2]

Pressures from societal culture make it increasingly difficult for each parent to be as involved as they would like in a child's activities. For example, schools often send newsletters, e-mails, and information to one parent instead of both, effectively screening out the other parent from participating in parent-teacher conferences, field trips, sports, concerts, and any other events in which the child is involved. This is not deliberate, but it's a bureaucratic norm that forces one parent to keep the other informed about the child's activities—something that isn't always likely to happen regularly or in a timely manner. This can result in one parent coming to every event while the other is effectively left out. All these conflicting occurrences in a child's life can communicate that one parent is more interested than the other, and that one parent is more at fault than the other in creating the need for divorce.

When you are struggling with the day-to-day realities of divorce—financial challenges, logistics, and operating as a single parent at least part of the time—it can be difficult to realize that your top priority, your children, may have slid out of focus. It's important to check in with your children to find out how they are dealing with all these changes, and to let them know how much you care about them. Demonstrate to them that you are open to talk about anything they like. Plan a family afternoon or evening when you and your children do a craft project at home or have a movie night with ice cream. You do not need to be extravagant—you need to be available, and you need to reassure your children that you love them and are ready to listen to them.

....

2.   Jennifer Lewis and William Sammons, "Looking at Divorce—Through the Eyes of a Child," ChildrenandDivorce.com, accessed January 15, 2014, http://www .childrenanddivorce.com/id18.html.

Signs of Emotional Distress

Parents tend to wait until their children exhibit signs of stress or inappropriate behavior before they believe that their children may be having difficulty coping with the upheaval in their lives. To delay addressing children's issues with the divorce, however, can mean greater and more damaging changes when the stress finally surfaces.

Before your child acts out or descends into depression, connect with a mental-health professional who can be a sounding board for your child. A social worker or therapist who specializes in children and families can give your child a safe place to vent her frustrations, and to ask questions she might not feel she can ask you. Working with a mental health professional, your child can develop coping skills that she can't get from you while your own life has turned upside down. You will do your child a great service by providing a neutral space and the guidance of a caring and impartial adult.

If the conflict in your home has gone on for some time before you and your spouse finally decided to divorce, your child already may have developed behavioral or emotional problems. Some of the signs of these issues include:

- **Falling grades:** When a good student suddenly loses interest in school, or the teacher reports that homework assignments are not being completed, it's a sure sign that something else is on the child's mind.

- **Outbursts of anger:** Children often have not yet developed constructive ways to express frustration and anger, so they keep quiet until they seem to explode with rage.

- **Aggressive behavior:** Stemming directly from anger issues, children may pummel a classmate, throw toys or rocks, hit or kick another child at the playground without provocation, or punch or break objects.

- **Withdrawing from the family:** Your child may spend a lot more time alone in her room than she did before the divorce.

- **Withdrawing from friends at school:** If a naturally social child suddenly has no plans with friends for weeks at a time or drops out of extracurricular activities, she could be responding to pent-up anger and stress.

- **Silence around the house:** Your child may decide that it's better to say nothing at all than to tell you what's on her mind. She may stop answering questions, refuse to respond to your inquiries about her time with the other parent, and ignore you when you are in the room with her.

- **Insomnia:** A child who has trouble sleeping night after night has more on her mind than she can handle. Check with your pediatrician to rule out a medical problem, and talk with your child to find out what goes through her mind when she's alone in the dark.

- **Depression:** More than moping around the house, clinical depression brings a sense of hopelessness and despair that can be crippling to a child or an adult. If your child seems to be taking the divorce particularly hard, has crying bouts, seems listless and disinterested in any activities, and loses her sense of fun, she may be experiencing depression.

- **Anxiety:** Your child may have panic attacks involving shortness of breath, dizziness, shaking hands, stomach pain, and other symptoms. These can be accompanied by irrational fears of everyday things, such as riding in the car or leaving the house. While there may be no physical problem, your child is not "faking it"—her symptoms are real and very frightening to her.

- **Substance abuse:** Drugs and alcohol can seem like easy, fast routes to escape a bad situation, so it's not uncommon for older children to seek out these types of temporary remedies to ease their stress and unhappiness.

- **Cutting or eating disorders:** Some of the most insidious behavioral problems in young people stem from anger directed inward. If your child starts losing weight and refusing to eat, you need to seek professional help as soon as you can. If you see strange scars on arms or legs or find a razor blade or other weapon in a back-pack or bedroom, bloody tissues or a bloodstained washcloth, or other signs of treatment of a wound, a meeting with a doctor or a psychologist is your best recourse.[3]

If you see any of these symptoms of stress, anxiety, and anger, it's time to talk with your child and find out what she's thinking and feeling. You may hear things that are painful for you, particularly if she is angry with you for your role in making these changes happen. You may feel as though your child can't understand what happened to cause the divorce, or that she doesn't know how hard it's been on you. This is *not* the time to say, "You think it's hard on you? You can't possibly know how tough this is for me," or anything else that will make your child feel guilty for expressing her feelings. Your child needs to be honest with you, so do your best to listen and help her express herself. Understand that your child's reaction to divorce is much like grief. There's been an enormous change in the life she knew, and she may not like the way her new life is turning out.

When a child expresses stress or frustration as a result of a divorce, it is also not the time to throw that expression in your ex-spouse's face. Blaming your ex for your child's stress is exactly what your child fears you will do, and it is likely one of the reasons she has not expressed herself up to this point: She does not want to cause any more friction between her parents by admitting that she struggles to cope with your divorce. Instead of chastising your child or your ex-spouse, this is the time to say to your child, "I understand how you feel, because I feel a lot of that, too. I'm glad you've told me, so we can think about how to get through this together." Understand that you can't fix everything with one conversation. In the coming days, however, you can begin to address your child's stress and anxiety by eliminating some of the behaviors that cause the stress in the first place.

....

3. Kemp et al., "Children and Divorce."

Ten Ways to Address Your Child's Need for Security

1. **Make sure your child understands the reason for the divorce as you've presented it.** Since the first time you told your child that you and your spouse were splitting up, he may have heard an argument or seen behavior that made him think there's a darker, hidden reason—one that might even have something to do with him. Reassure him that the issue is as you said it is.

2. **Tell your child you love him.** Parents can forget to do this in the midst of other issues, but your child needs to know that while your love for your spouse is gone, you still love your children and always will.

3. **Establish schedules and routines.** The sooner your child's home life normalizes, the faster he will get past the initial turmoil and upheaval of the divorce. Routine establishes what comes next in a child's life, whether it's in the next hour or the next month. It can be very comforting as he tries to make sense of the changes in his life.

4. **Don't complain about your spouse to your child.** Complain to your friends, your counselor, your attorney, or whomever else you depend on for support, but not to your child. He still has a loving relationship with his other parent, and he doesn't want to hear the bad things you have to say. Nor should he ever be made to feel that he must be loyal to one parent or the other—this only makes things more difficult for him.

5. **Try to get along with your ex-spouse.** It will be much easier on your children, your friends, and each other if you establish a friendly relationship as quickly as you can. Your lives will intersect for many years to come, so you might as well get used to it sooner rather than later.

6. **Remember that your child is your child, not your friend.** It's never a good idea to dump all your problems in your child's lap as if he were a buddy. Your child may feel that he needs to solve your problems, or he may determine that he's the biggest problem you have. This is not a healthy relationship to have with a parent.

7. **Check in.** Talk to your child more than once about the divorce and his relationship with you and with his other parent. Make certain that he understands any new changes that have happened, that you love him, and that he has not decided that he is somehow responsible for your split. You may have said it ten times, but it might be the eleventh time that finally sinks in.

8. **Ask for your child's opinion about the visitation schedule.** The schedules and parameters for visitation may make sense in a settlement agreement or a courtroom, but they may seem utterly ridiculous to your child. If he's old enough to have extracurricular activities and friendships, check with him to see if you have created schedule conflicts that you may not have noticed. Make sure that being at one residence or the other on a given day does not mean that he will have to give up an activity he loves. It's not fair to set everything up for your convenience and then force your child to accept the arrangement without any input.

9. **Speak directly to your ex-spouse, rather than sending messages through your child.** Your child feels like a pawn in a stressful game when he carries information from one parent to another, especially if that information raises the other parent's ire. Few things are harder on your child than being told by an angry parent, "Oh yeah? Well, you tell your father that I said ..." Don't put your child through this; even if you know you're going to have a tense exchange with your spouse, pick up the phone or send a text and deliver your own messages.

10. **Tell the school, your child's doctors, and others to send information to both spouses.** When one parent stops coming to games, concerts, plays, or other events in which the child is involved, your child begins to think that the absent parent

doesn't care about him anymore. If you are the custodial parent, make a point of providing your spouse's contact information to the school, the coaches, and others who lead the extracurricular activities in which your child is involved. You may want to make your spouse appear unfeeling and disinterested, but that's not fair to your child.[4]

....

4. Jocelyn Block and Melinda Smith, "Tips for Divorced Parents: Co-parenting with Your Ex and Making Joint Custody Work," HelpGuide.org, last modified December 2013, http://www.helpguide.org/mental/coparenting_shared_parenting_divorce.htm.

CHAPTER SIX

Custody and Child Support

The phrase you will hear over and over as you work out a child custody agreement with your spouse is "in the best interests of the child." This goal takes precedence over all others as you, your mediator or attorneys, and the court consider how your relationship with your children will continue as your marriage ends. What exactly these "best interests" are will depend on a number of factors, including the children's preferences, you and your spouse's personal health and lifestyle, and the ability of each of you to support a standard of living that benefits your child while keeping him safe and healthy.

If you and your spouse see eye to eye on the subject of custody, you don't need to use the court system to hammer out the details. Working together with a mediator, you can create a custody agreement, set up a visitation or joint custody schedule, and bring the matter to a swift resolution. If you disagree on the terms of custody, however, you may need to take the matter to court—which means that you will spend time not only on creating a case for yourself as a stellar parent, but also on proving that your spouse is not a fit custodian for your child. This process can be contentious and can severely damage the relationship you have with your spouse—one you need to maintain as you continue to be parents to your child.

To fully understand the challenge or compromise that may be ahead, you will need a firm grasp of child custody laws.

Understanding Custody and Child Support

When considering a child custody case, the court will take a number of factors into consideration. These include:

- the age and health of the child

- the emotional bond between the child and each parent

- which parent has been the primary caregiver to the child

- how much time each parent spends with the child

- any history of violence, physical abuse, substance abuse, and other dangers

- the child's current living environment and its safety

- in some states, exposure to secondhand smoke

- each parent's employment situation and ability to take care of the child

- the child's own preference for living with one parent over the other, if the child is at least twelve years old

- potential disruption to the child's established routine, and the best way to minimize inconvenience and change in the child's life

- the child's choice of religion, if the child is twelve years old or older and the parents are from different faiths or disagree on the religion in which the child should be raised[1]

On the issue of religion, courts in most states will look closely at the potential for "actual or substantial harm," or the risk of such harm to the child if he or she is raised in a specific religion. If no harm is indicated and the child is under twelve years old, the court will most likely defer to

....

1. "How Will the Court Decide My Child Custody Case?," CADivorce.com, accessed January 15, 2014, http://www.cadivorce.com/california-divorce-guide/child-custody -and-visitation/how-will-the-court-decide-my-child-custody-case/.

the First Amendment right of the custodial parent to raise the child in that parent's religion of choice. There are exceptions to this general rule in just about every state, however, so if religion is an important point in your custody case, you may need to build a particularly strong case to put one parent's First Amendment right over the other.[2]

Getting a Temporary Order of Custody

When you and your spouse first decide to divorce, you do not necessarily have the right to take your children and move out of the house. Before you grab the kids and leave, the court has to grant you temporary custody, recognizing that you will be the custodial parent until your divorce-settlement agreement has been finalized.

Your temporary order of custody will establish either of you as having primary custody, as well as set the visitation arrangement for the other parent. At the same time, you can file for a temporary order to determine the amount of child support the noncustodial parent will pay to the custodial parent to feed, clothe, and house the children. Generally, the custodial spouse will be given temporary possession of the family home as well, to maintain a level of normalcy in the children's lives.

Even if you have not yet filed your petition for divorce, you can already apply for temporary custody. If you and your spouse can agree on a custody arrangement for the time being while you sort out the details of your divorce, you can fill out some paperwork and submit this agreement to the court for approval. This makes your arrangement legal and binding until it is superseded by your divorce decree.

If you can't agree on a custody arrangement on your own, you can have a judge make the decision for you. The courts put the safety and welfare of your children first—just as you are doing by addressing this issue promptly—so your case can be fast-tracked and heard by a judge within a few days. You will fill out an *order to show cause* (OSC), a basic document that defines the order for which you are asking. This document sets a date and time for your hearing, and orders your spouse to

....

2. "Child Custody and Religion," Nolo.com, accessed January 15, 2014, http://www .nolo.com/legal-encyclopedia/child-custody-religion-29887.html.

come and "show cause" for why you should or should not be granted this temporary custody.

In addition to the OSC, you will submit your own testimony in writing, explaining why you need this and any other temporary orders. If other people are involved and have firsthand testimony to share, you can submit statements from them in writing as well. You or your attorney will also draw up a proposed temporary order, which the judge will sign in court if it is approved.

You will need to make certain that a copy of each of these documents is delivered to your spouse, and prove this to the court according to the laws of your state. Consult your attorney or see your state's divorce laws page online to be sure this is done properly. If you are asking for child support, be sure to bring proof of your income and expenses when you appear in court (or in the judge's chambers). In some states, you will need to file documents with your request for the temporary order so that the judge can review them in advance of your hearing.

During the hearing, the judge may ask questions of you and your spouse (if he or she attends) and will make an immediate decision on your order request. This will establish one of the parents as having primary custody until the divorce becomes final. It does not necessarily mean that you or your spouse will have permanent custody, or that you can restrict your spouse's access to your children indefinitely. All of these issues will come up again as you complete your divorce-settlement agreement.

In a few cases, the judge may determine that he or she does not have enough information to make a decision on temporary custody, so you will need to work with your attorney to gather the missing documentation. The judge also may decide that your spouse did not have enough notice to prepare adequately for the hearing, so another hearing will be scheduled for several days or weeks down the road. If this is the case, the judge will grant an order that provides a custody arrangement that is the least disruptive to the children, but it will only be in effect until the next hearing.[3]

....

3. "Temporary Orders in Family Court: Quick Decisions on Support and Custody," Nolo.com, accessed January 15, 2014, http://www.nolo.com/legal-encyclopedia /temporary-orders-family-court-29642.html.

Fitness for Parenthood

The natural parents of the child are both considered fit to serve as the custodial parent by the court, unless there is tangible proof—what the courts call *substantial competent evidence*—that shows otherwise. What this means exactly can differ from one state to another, one court to another, and even from one judge to another, making it very difficult to determine an individual judge's requirements for substantial evidence.

If you believe that your spouse is an unfit parent, you will need to work closely with a child custody attorney to determine what the judge in your case will consider proof. Your attorney should know how other cases by this particular judge have been decided, and whether your evidence has enough substance to potentially convince the judge that your soon-to-be ex-spouse should not have primary or joint custody of your child.

Once you and your spouse have decided to divorce, every action the both of you take can have a direct impact on your custody case. If you move out of the family home and leave your children with your spouse, for example, the court can consider this an endorsement on your part of your spouse's fitness as a parent. If leaving them with your spouse means that the children continue to live in the same place and attend the same schools, the judge may determine that the healthiest situation for the children is the one with the least possible disruption to their lives. In this case, the parent with whom the children are living would become the custodial parent almost by default.

While laws in many states once awarded children aged five and under to the mother automatically, these laws have been mostly eliminated. Today the fitness of both parents is taken into account, and custody decisions are made based on what is best for the child. Custody may be determined by which parent has more time at home or which has flexible work hours—as well as by mental and physical health and the ability to provide a safe environment for the child.

Types of Child Custody

Specific child custody laws differ from state to state, but you will generally see four kinds of child custody recognized:

1. **Sole physical custody:** The children live with one parent all the time, and the other parent has specific visitation rights. "Physical" custody refers to the parent with whom the children actually live.

2. **Joint (or shared) physical custody:** The children will have continuous contact with both parents, living part time with one parent and part with another. This often results in a split-week or alternate-week schedule, though children may live with each parent for alternate months or even years.

3. **Sole legal custody:** One parent makes decisions about the education, health, and overall welfare of the child, while the other parent has a specific visitation schedule. This is the most common arrangement recognized by the courts across the country, according to LegalZoom.[4]

4. **Joint (or shared) legal custody:** Both parents have the right to make decisions about the children's health and welfare. The parents submit a parenting plan to the court and share the decision-making regarding the children's education, health care, and daily life. This form of custody can only work if the parents commit to maintaining an amicable relationship.

In three of the four kinds of child custody, visitation becomes a major question. The laws on visitation vary from state to state, but they do agree on this much: "Any person having an interest in the children's welfare is entitled to reasonable visitation."[5] This means that other relatives, including grandparents, also have to be taken into consideration

....

4. "Custody of Minor Children in a Divorce," LegalZoom.com, accessed January 15, 2014. http://www.legalzoom.com/divorce-guide/custody-of-minor-children.html.
5. Ibid.

and scheduled for visitation, especially when they are family members of the noncustodial parent.

While joint physical custody arrangements can be costly (each parent maintains a residence with room for the children), such a custody agreement does allow both parents to be involved in the children's lives on a regular basis. Schedules can become complicated, but after a period of trial and error, these issues can become routine. Each parent can plan on time off from the day-to-day demands of raising children, and some find that it provides them with free time they can look forward to on a regular basis.

As you move forward with a joint custody agreement, keep in mind that you and your spouse will need to maintain at least a cordial relationship, so that you can discuss schedule changes, your children's expenses, health issues, and other events that might disrupt the normal routine. Keeping the lines of communication open between you will help your children understand that they can be safe and happy with either of you, even in two different residences. When you can smile and be civil to one another, your children will have no reason to believe that they are too much trouble to you, or that they have somehow caused the rift that split you up.

Calculating Child Support

In any divorce involving minor children, the noncustodial spouse is required to pay child support to the spouse who is raising the children. How much child support must be paid depends on the laws of your state. Every state has its own formula for child support, and some of them can be very complicated. Your state has a calculator online that will allow you to get an estimate of what you might be expected to pay in child support, or how much you may expect from your spouse. Check the "Child Support Calculators" page at AllLaw.com (http://www .alllaw.com/calculators/childsupport/) for a link to the calculator for your state.

Most states calculate child support based on the income of the noncustodial parent, while some also look at the income of the spouse with primary custody. What exactly "income" means can change from one state to another: Your state may use gross income, net income, overtime, and bonuses in the calculation of your monthly support payment. Your state may consider one or more of these variables as well:

- the amount of alimony you or your spouse may be paying for a previous marriage

- the time that each parent spends with the children

- the cost of day care, and who pays for it

- the cost of health insurance and medical expenses

- if the children have specific educational needs—for example, if a child is developmentally disabled and needs a full-time aide or a special school program

- travel expenses required for visitation

- if either parent supports children from a previous marriage

- any deductions from either spouse's paycheck for union dues or other professional costs

- the children's ages

- any lump-sum payments you or your spouse may receive from an employer, a second job, or any other source

- investment income either of you may have in addition to your employment income

- whether you or your spouse has a new partner who lives in the residence and contributes to the household income[6]

Once weekly or monthly payments have been established, either parent can ask for modifications of the child support order whenever they feel that change is warranted. For example, if the noncustodial parent has a significant negative change in income, he or she can request that the amount of child support be lowered. If the child's expenses

....

6. "Child Support in a Divorce," LegalZoom.com, accessed February 3, 2014, http://www.legalzoom.com/divorce-guide/divorce-child-support.html.

increase because the parents have decided that the child should attend a private school, the custodial spouse may request additional child support from the other to help cover this cost.

If either parent requests a change in the child support amount, the change will be made only if both parents agree on the new payment amount. They also must agree that the new amount is in the child's best interest, and that it will meet the new need as stated by the custodial parent.

Whether or not you believe that a recalculation of child support may be in your future, be sure to keep all your receipts from your child's expenses as well as careful records of what you spend on a weekly and monthly basis for your child's food, clothing, shelter, health, and education. This will make it much easier for you to defend the amount of child support paid or received should you find yourself back in court over the size of the payments.

Tips for Interacting with Your Child's Other Parent

One of the hardest things to deal with after a divorce is the continued relationship you must maintain with your ex-spouse while you share parenting responsibilities. It's only natural for feelings of anger, resentment, betrayal, and frustration to come through long after the divorce decree is signed, even after all legal personnel have faded into the past. You want to get on with your life, and you want to continue the loving relationship you have with your kids, but you need to tolerate the person whom you may still blame for the new level of complication in your life.

As much as you might feel the urge to argue about the differences that led to your divorce, that part of your marriage is over. Just as the courts hold "the best interests of the child" as their top priority, so should you—which means that you and your ex-spouse need to develop an understanding when it comes to your continued communication.

In most cases, your children still want to have you as an integral part of their lives, whether you are the custodial parent, you're sharing joint physical custody, or you see them on a visitation schedule. Do your best to find a way to put the pain of your divorce behind you so that you can focus on your children and be the parent they need you to be.

This is not to say that you will never encounter bumps in the road as you and your ex-spouse confer on things that need to be done for your children. Even if you were still happily married, you would have disagreements—this is a normal thing in any relationship. How you handle these differences, however, can have a huge impact on how bearable the relationship is. Whether it's a scheduling conflict or a decision on the right school, you can choose to sit down and figure out a reasonable solution without descending into accusations and harsh words.

You will get a great deal of advice from your divorced friends about how to treat your ex, but you need to find what works for you. Here are some of the guidelines recommended by counselors and other experts in the field of spousal communication:[7]

- **Think about your kids.** The whole reason you continue to have conversations with your ex is to discuss your children and something they need. Keeping this at the forefront of your mind can help you avoid a confrontation.

- **Think before you speak.** Your first impulse may be to lash out. Don't say the first thing that pops into your head; think about a way to take the anger out of the words.

- **Be the bigger person.** Your ex-spouse may take a cheap shot at you, but you don't have to respond in kind—and you're the stronger person if you choose to ignore a verbal jab. Continue the conversation calmly, and your ex-spouse will have the choice of matching your tone or looking foolish.

....

7. Block and Smith, "Co-parenting with Your Ex"; Laura Markham, "Divorce: Protecting Your Kids," AhaParenting.com, accessed January 15, 2014, http://www .ahaparenting.com/parenting-tools/family-life/Divorce-protecting-kids; and Kristen Wynns, "Dealing with Divorce: 10 Tips to Protect Your Kids," WynnsFamilyPsychology .com, accessed January 15, 2014, http://wynnsfamilypsychology.com/Dealingwith Divorce10TipstoProtectYourKids/tabid/760/language/en-US/Default.aspx.

- **Have the conversation where your kids can't see or hear you.**
  If there's any chance that an issue will escalate into a fight, try to discuss it where you won't make your children feel like the cause of your trouble.

- **Don't complain to your kids.** As discussed in chapter 5, your children are not equipped to process your complaints about your ex-spouse. If you need to vent, talk to a friend or counselor but not to your children.

- **Find a different outlet.** Rather than arguing with your ex, try going to the gym, hopping onto the elliptical trainer in your den, or taking a brisk walk. In fifteen to twenty minutes, you will have done something healthy and your anger will have dissipated.

- **Break the stress cycle.** Recognize the symptoms of stress: rapid breathing, pounding heart, angry feelings, shaking hands—or silence and difficulty keeping your thoughts straight. Whatever your specific stress reactions, you can break the cycle even when you're in the middle of a heated discussion. Change your thoughts: Think of a favorite place or of a quiet walk in the woods or about the words to a favorite song. Have a place in your home that you can disappear to for a few minutes to calm your nerves. Light a scented candle. Once the stressful discussion ends, get outside and take a walk, or phone a friend to "talk you down."

- **Be consistent.** Your child now lives in two houses, and it's easy to imagine that she will have one set of rules in your home and another with your ex. Each of you has a different parenting style, and there's nothing wrong with that—but it's good to establish at least a few rules that cross both thresholds. Bedtime, no video games until homework is done, and basic standards for behavior are things you and your ex can establish together.

- **Admit when you're wrong.** If something you've done is messing up the family schedule, apologize before asking your ex-spouse for a change of plans. An apology can work like magic when it comes to diminishing angry feelings.

- **Ask your ex-spouse for help.** If your child is acting out at school, it's a problem for both parents, and you both need to be involved in addressing the issue with your child. Share your concerns with your ex-spouse and engage his or her assistance. Your child still has two parents, so you don't need to go it alone (or to feel resentful that this is happening during your time with your child).

- **Let things go.** Sometimes your child will return home a little later than planned, or there will be a special event that requires more time than one of you expected. Chances are that your spouse did not keep the child out late to be vindictive toward you. If the first thing your child sees is you fighting with your spouse over a late arrival, your child will feel guilty and the special time she just had will be ruined. Pick your battles carefully.

Ten Things to Consider When Making Decisions about Your Children

Lastly, here is a list of suggestions to consider when you are making decisions about your children:

1. **Make an agreement with your ex-spouse that your children are your first priority.** It can't be said often enough that your children come before the anger or resentment you and your ex-spouse feel toward one another. When you remain focused on your children and their emotional well-being, many other decisions will fall into place.

2. **Ask what your child wants.** If you have several children, they may each have their own attitude about your divorce and the visitation schedule. Make sure they are all heard, and take their concerns seriously. It may be easy to fix a particular issue—like making sure a favorite stuffed animal always gets packed to go visit the other spouse. If a child does not want to go to see the

other parent, probe gently to find out why, and see if you can talk through the problem with the child or your ex.

3. **Don't make your kids choose between you.** It's one thing to ask your child how he feels about your divorce, but it's quite another to try to corner him into telling you which parent he likes better. If every day is a contest between the two parents, you've created an untenable situation for your child.

4. **Figure out how to keep your home life as normal as possible.** Keep your child's schedule of after-school activities, visits to grandparents, play dates with friends, and all the other things that feel normal and predictable. If most aspects of his life keep their usual routine, you will go a long way in making him feel secure again.

5. **Remember that you got divorced, not your kids.** Your children still seek an active relationship with both parents, even though one of you no longer lives in the house. In most cases, the children still love the other parent; they do not share the animosity you feel for your ex-spouse and they don't want the changes that have been imposed on them. They expect their relationship with the other parent to go on as it always has, and they deserve that. The better you both can facilitate this relationship, the healthier your children will be within the divorce.

6. **Stay involved in your child's life.** Whether or not you are sharing joint custody, your children need two parents in their lives. This means that the both of you need to attend the children's school events and other activities, just as you would if you were still married. If you are sharing custody, then neither of you is a single parent—and you both need to parent your child.

7. **Realize that in some cases, an absent parent is better than a negative parent.** Studies consistently show that a child whose parent becomes completely absent creates less stress than a parent who is constantly harsh and negative with the child. If your spouse has abandoned you and your children, your child

has a better chance of healing and moving on than he does if your spouse remains in the picture and criticizes everything your child does or says.

8. **Contact a child therapist before stress gets out of hand.** It's long past time to put the stigma of mental distress on the shelf. If you wait until you see the signs of stress in your children, they could already be deep into self-destructive behaviors or patterns of thought that wear away at their self-esteem. Talk to their school counselor or find a private practice that can help you link your child with a caring adult who can lend an impartial ear.

9. **Pay your child support.** If you are the noncustodial parent, make the payments on time. Not doing so punishes your children, not your ex-spouse; the lack of money can threaten their health and the roof over their heads.

10. **Don't demand that your children act like adults.** Your kids are still kids, and they need you to be the adult in their relationship with you. They are not there to take care of you or comfort you; that is your role in the family. Telling your six-year-old son, "You're the man in the family now," puts an extraordinary amount of pressure on a child who is nowhere near ready for it. Maintain your role and be the grown-up in the relationship.

PART THREE

Divorce and Your Emotions

CHAPTER SEVEN

Dealing with Emotions

Divorce hurts. There's simply no way around that pain. You believed that you had married your spouse for life, that you would be together no matter what, and that you would never have to face another night alone or day without companionship and love. Yet here you are, feeling like you've been slapped in the face and punched in the stomach at the same time.

People will ask you if you've "gotten past it," but there's no timetable for recovering from the shock and anger that can come with divorce. You will need to find your own way through the pain on your own time, no matter how many of your friends suggest that you should be "over it" by now. Every aspect of your life has changed: your relationship status, your economic security, your position in your children's lives, even your daily schedule. On top of all the disruption and upheaval, you need to cope with the fact that you no longer love the person you married, and he or she no longer loves you—or if you do still love your spouse, you have to adjust to the idea that he or she paid someone a lot of money to arrange an agreement that ended your marriage.

More than anything else, you probably just want to feel normal again—whatever that may mean now. The process of returning to a sense of normalcy, routine, and self-confidence differs with every person, but it can be done. In this chapter, you'll learn about ways to cope with the massive changes in your life, and begin to rebuild your self-esteem and sense of worth.

Coping with the Decision

What went wrong? What did I do? What could I have done differently? How will I ever feel happy again? These and dozens of other questions race through your mind, especially at night when you wish you could escape into sleep. Even if your spouse has addressed most of these questions, the answers are hardly satisfying—in fact, they may only cause more pain. If you blame yourself, your thoughts can be unbearably sad; if you blame your spouse, the anger and sense of betrayal threaten to overwhelm you.

The only thing to do is to take your life one day at a time, or even one hour at a time if a day seems too long to handle. Give yourself the time you need to step back from the emotional turmoil—something you will not be able to do right away—and determine what you need each day in order to get from one hour to the next. What you need may be completely different from the needs your friends had when they went through divorce, but their advice and insights may be helpful. Your good friend's story about the cathartic effect of throwing away all her spouse's toiletries may provide you with a good laugh, as well as the understanding that your anger, resentment, pain, and grief are a common part of the recovery process.

It's incredibly easy to fall into the trap of guilt, isolation, and martyrdom as you start down the path as a single adult. You may be tempted to lock yourself in your bedroom until the worst feelings pass, but removing yourself from your social network and your daily responsibilities will only deepen your feelings of loneliness and anger. You need friends, though you may need to carefully choose who will become your closest confidants during this difficult time. Choose the ones who will help you climb out of the lonely abyss, not the ones who will drag you down further by rekindling your fury. Equally important is reassessing your social life to determine which friends you "got" in the divorce, and which people will probably pull back from you now. (More on this in chapter 8.)

At the same time, you have a long list of practical issues to consider. You need to reorganize your financial life as a single person, taking stock of what you have and what you will need to do to fill in the gap left by your spouse's income. You need to continue to perform well at your job, despite the turmoil in your home life. You need to normalize your children's schedules and make them feel that they have a safe home—or two safe homes—and that you will support them emotionally as well as physically. All of these activities can help you shift your focus away from the emotional pain of your divorce. Embrace the busy work as a useful distraction as well as a necessity, giving yourself the opportunity to think about something more than the big hole left by the end of your marriage.

If you find that your guilt, grief, and anger are lingering longer than you ever imagined, seek a counselor who works with people going through divorce. There's no reason to suffer in silence. A good counselor will be able to help you rediscover your self-esteem and begin to move past the anger and guilt. He or she also can work with your primary care physician to recommend the use of medications for clinical depression and anxiety, two mental health issues that often accompany divorce. Medications like these are not a crutch, and you're not "popping pills"; they are types of treatment for temporary medical conditions that have been caused or exacerbated by the turmoil in your life.

The Emotional Stages of Divorce

In 1969, the Swiss author Elisabeth Kübler-Ross wrote her first book on the process of coping with death, *On Death and Dying*, for which she interviewed hundreds of people who were facing the end of their lives. She developed a theory that has stood the test of time for more than forty years, in which she determined the five stages of grief people experience when they know that death is approaching.[1]

These five stages—denial, anger, bargaining, depression, and acceptance—apply to divorce just as remarkably as they do to death.[2]

....

1. Elisabeth Kübler-Ross, *On Death and Dying: What the Dying Have to Teach Doctors, Nurses, Clergy, and Their Own Families* (New York: Scribner Classics, 1997), 51–146.

2. Cathy Meyer, "The Emotional Stages of Divorce: What to Expect during and after the Divorce Process," *Huffington Post,* November 8, 2010, http://www.huffingtonpost.com/cathy-meyer/the-emotional-stages-of-d_b_779816.html.

While Kübler-Ross herself noted that these stages are not always sequential and can often overlap, the general sense is the same: You will travel through these emotional stages at your own pace, eventually able to accept your situation for what it is.

1. **Denial:** At first, the fact that your marriage is ending will seem surreal or even unreal, and you will find a tremendous capacity for pretending that it's not happening. The signs are there, and perhaps your spouse has even announced that he or she wants to proceed with a divorce, but you are convinced that if you just keep your head down and power through, all this will go back to normal. You can stay in this stage for quite some time before the divorce petition arrives and you have no choice but to move forward with the inevitable.

    If you are the spouse choosing to get the divorce, you may already have been through the denial stage—one that kept you from making this move months or even years earlier. You, too, know the sweet deception of going through the motions on a daily basis, pretending that nothing is amiss and that you and your spouse are "just in a phase" or "past all that romance stuff." At some point, however, you became ready to take the next step. Chances are that something in particular set you off, enabling you to move to the anger stage, where action takes place.

2. **Anger:** You thought you might get through this divorce without rage and outbursts, but you were wrong. Suddenly everything that's the matter with your life is your spouse's fault, and you want him or her to know it. A phone call that's a moment late becomes a monumental injustice; a change in your carefully planned schedule with your children takes on the importance of a murder case. If you haven't filed for divorce yet, this may be the time that you actually fill out the paperwork and deliver it to court.

    You are entitled to your anger and there's no avoiding it, but remember that your children do not need to become involved. You may feel an irrepressible urge to humiliate your spouse in front of your kids or to berate your children for their loyalty to their other parent, but you will regret doing this for months or years to come. Not only will your relationship with your spouse sustain lasting damage, but your children will be put in the untenable situation of dividing their loyalties between the two of you—an impossible and emotionally damaging task. Your momentary satisfaction is not worth their emotional well-being.

3. **Bargaining:** When the pain and depression become more than you believe you can bear, you begin to think, *I have to fix this, because I just can't take feeling like this anymore.* Suddenly your spouse seems like the most attractive, most lovable person you ever knew, and you feel a tremendous need to mend fences and put your lives back together. Whatever went on between you before you decided to split up, it seems infinitely better than this life of loneliness and grief in which you find yourself now. Chances are that you will move through this stage fairly quickly, especially if your attempts to bargain your way back into your spouse's life fail miserably. Remember that your spouse will go through this stage as well, so if there is a reconciliation in your future, it's possible that you will both realize its merits at the same time.

4. **Depression:** When it becomes clear that you and your spouse will never be together again, you may sink into a period of minimal functioning, when your days will be spent going through the motions at work and your nights find you in front of the TV watching the Lifetime channel or ESPN. Insomnia or too much sleeping, lack of interest in hygiene, loss of appetite, lots of crying, and isolation are all part of this stage, especially if there are no children to keep you moving and force you to leave the house on occasion. This is when you need your friends, your counselor, and your family members (if they are supportive and do not add to your already towering pile of blame) to help you move through this dark, terribly sad stage. Friends who have been through divorce—or even a bad breakup— know what's coming, and may surprise you with their ability to understand what you're experiencing.

5. **Acceptance:** Oh happy day when the depression slips away and you can see the sun again! You thought this day would never

come, but it's here, and you have the first feelings of optimism about your new life. It's not that you will never have another day of anger or sadness—those days will come—but that you will be less shattered by them and more willing to look constructively at problems and find workable solutions. The worst is over, and you have survived it.

Keep in mind that your process belongs to you, and while others can share their experiences and give you some insights, they cannot tell you how to get past your own emotional turmoil. *There is no right or wrong way to grieve.* Your situation will share some things in common with others, and be completely different at the same time; you will move through the process and find your coping strategies in your own way.

Handling Stress

On top of the emotional turmoil and the legal and logistical issues that come with divorce, you are most likely questioning all kinds of things about your new life. Can you get by on your own, without your spouse's financial contribution? Can you manage a household and succeed as a parent? Can you help your children feel safe and loved in a divided marriage? Will your in-laws still treat you like a member of the family when they visit with your children? Can you keep up with your work now that you have greater responsibilities at home?

You need to build an arsenal of techniques to cope with the stress of building a new life without your spouse. Find a few things that work for you, and make a point of fitting them into your schedule as often as possible. It may be that you need to wait until the very end of the day, after your children are in bed, to take the time for yourself—but even a few minutes a day can help you reduce the agitation you feel as you create your new life. Here are some additional approaches to alleviating stress:

- **Join a support group.** It's a great way to get out of the house and meet others who are experiencing the same things you are.

- **Make plans with friends.** It's easy to let your relationships slide when you have so much to do every day, but your social network is critical to your sense of self-esteem and well-being. Don't give yourself the opportunity to think, *No one wants to be with me.*

- **Don't worry about quid pro quo with your friends and family.** If a pal brings over a takeout dinner to share with you and your kids, you don't have to run out and do the same for them a couple of nights later. Your friends want to help, just as you would if the situation were reversed. These things balance out over the course of a friendship.

- **Give yoga a try.** Yoga and other simple stretching and breathing techniques can release a lot of the stress your body carries throughout the day. If you feel stiffness in your shoulders, aching in your legs, and back pain that you never had before the divorce, half an hour's worth of yoga can help.

- **Throw away things you don't need.** Get the clutter out of your house, especially if it includes things your spouse left behind. If you don't want it, lose it. The extra space you gain gives you room for the new things in your life.

- **Give yourself a break.** This is not the time to go on a diet, train for a marathon, learn a foreign language, or overhaul your house's electrical system. Do just what you need to do until you find your footing in your new life. All of those projects will still be there when you're ready.

- **Take big tasks a piece at a time.** If you are decorating your daughter's new bedroom, for example, take one evening to mask all the molding and another to paint the walls, and a third to put up pictures and decals. If you are doing your own income taxes for the first time, give yourself a week to pull all the documents together, and another to choose tax software and learn to use it. Breaking down the task into smaller chunks will make the work seem far less daunting.

- **Take a positive step forward.** One of your big tasks may be to retrain for your reentry into the workforce. Sitting down to do your homework while your child does hers can create a new kind of bond, while you set a tremendous example of diligence and responsibility. Going back to school can create plenty of stress, but it can also result in new income and independence you did not have before.[3]

Self-Care during Divorce

People often talk about being on the "divorce diet," a sudden, precipitous weight loss that takes place when they lost their appetite during their postdivorce depression. You may be thinking, *I should be so lucky!* This weight loss, however, only serves to illustrate the truth about the divorce process: It can set you up to neglect your health while you find your way through the darker times. Not only can a poor diet and lack of exercise make you feel unwell, it's also not a healthy example to set for your children. If you don't have kids, you still owe it to yourself to approach your new life with all the energy you can muster.

A balanced diet of protein, complex carbohydrates, fiber, and plenty of water will clear your head and keep your body functioning at peak efficiency. Meat, poultry, fish, fruits and vegetables, and other fresh foods are infinitely preferable over packaged frozen dinners that are loaded with sodium, fat, and sugar. If you must snack, choose whole-grain cookies and crackers and low-fat dairy products instead of grabbing a whole pint of fat-laden ice cream and a spoon.

Sunlight, fresh air, and open landscapes do wonders for the soul, and the sun actually provides much-needed vitamin D to your body. You don't have to be a daily jogger to enjoy half an hour outdoors—take your dog or your kids for a walk around your neighborhood, or for an

....

3. Jane Collingwood, "Reduce the Stress of a Divorce," PsychCentral.com, accessed January 16, 2014, http://psychcentral.com/lib/reduce-the-stress-of-a-divorce/0001003.

outing in a nearby park. The change of scenery can help you shift your focus away from all the things that trouble you.[4]

Exercise is like a tonic to your body, pumping blood through your veins and arteries to clear out the residue left by the pint of ice cream you gave in to and ate. Beyond the basic health benefits, exercise increases the levels of endorphins—powerful proteins that elevate mood—in your system. If you need a way to burn off feelings of aggression, try a martial arts or cardio kick class, or do some strength training with free weights or fitness machines. Joining a gym is a worthwhile expense if you have time to actually go to one; if not, get some exercise DVDs or record some workout programs on your DVR.

Reinventing your look can be tremendous fun as you begin to envision yourself meeting new people and even forming a new relationship. If a spa makeover is not within your budget, you can experiment at home with a new hairstyle and grooming techniques that revitalize your self-esteem. A change of wardrobe can make an important difference in the way you see yourself as well as the way others see you. Try a few things and see how they work, with the understanding that your look is sort of a hobby—it's something you can experiment with again and again.

Ten Techniques for Dealing with Emotions

Everyone goes through their own process of grief, and everyone deals with emotions differently. Still, there are things you can do to work through this difficult period. Here are some tips for coping when things get rough:

1. **Stop beating yourself up.** Rarely in the world has there been a divorce in which one spouse was completely culpable and the

....

4. "Dealing with Stress and Depression during Divorce and Separation," FamilyLives .org.uk, accessed January 16, 2014, http://familylives.org.uk/advice/divorce-and -separation/thinking-about-divorce/dealing-with-stress-and-depression-during -divorce-and-separation/.

other was blameless. You are not the only one at fault, and you need to stop accepting full responsibility for the breakup.

2. **Forgive and let go.** You can accuse your spouse all you want, but once your divorce is final, the damage wrought by your dying relationship has reached its end. Don't give your spouse all the power in your continued relationship, or all the real estate you're allowing your spouse to inhabit in your head. Look closely and find a way to put your anger aside. It's important that you not allow your past relationship to cloud your life going forward.

3. **Close the life script.** It's easy to decide that your behavior during your marriage and divorce are part of a pattern begun when you were a child, and that continuing this pattern is beyond your control. You certainly don't want to keep repeating past mistakes, but you need to understand that this repetition (if it actually exists) is neither inevitable nor uncontrollable.

4. **Stop thinking and do something.** Keeping yourself busy may seem like you're dodging the problem Scarlett O'Hara–style, but it's preferable to stewing endlessly on what's gone wrong in your life.

5. **Clean and unclutter your house.** Get rid of the things you no longer need, and scrub everything until it shines. You'll be amazed at the amount of space you gain and the way a sparkling-clean, dusted home improves your overall mood.

6. **Allow yourself to be less than perfect.** You have new responsibilities and you won't get every one of them right every time. This is normal, and it makes you human. Expect the occasional slipup and be ready for it. If you bounce a check, miss a credit card payment, drop off your child ten minutes late for his football practice, forget to return a phone call from your mother, or any of the other thousand-odd things that you might do wrong, forgive yourself. Correct the error if you can, and move on.

7. **Go out.** You won't be ready to date right away, but you have friends who enjoy your company—and there's nothing wrong with going to a movie by yourself if you wish. Being the custodial

parent does not mean that you can never do anything without your kids—and being the noncustodial parent doesn't mean you can only do things when your kids are with your spouse. Join a club, become more active in a favorite activity, do some volunteer work, or at the very least attend a support group meeting. It's time to return to the land of the living.

8. **Do something fun with your kids.** Whether it's playing a board game or a video game, baking cookies, or shooting hoops in the driveway, whatever your children enjoy can be fun for you, too (and you don't have to spend a fortune doing it). Your children know how to have a good time without trying very hard. Take a lesson from them and join them in an activity that will make you smile.

9. **Turn off Lifetime and watch comedies.** It may seem natural to seek out entertainment that reflects your mood, but why make it worse when the same amount of time and energy could make it better? There's nothing like some great physical comedy or the wit of a television sitcom to lift your spirits.

10. **Cut yourself some slack.** Some days will be better than others. You may have had several days or even weeks of relatively happy time, but then something triggers an emotional setback. This is a normal part of the healing process, and it will pass just as the pain and loss of your divorce eventually did. Acknowledge that this is a bad day, and that tomorrow you will wake up feeling better about yourself and your situation. The odds are that this will be true.

CHAPTER EIGHT

Dealing with Relationships

With all the changes that take place during a divorce, one of the hardest to deal with is the shift in the relationships you have known through the course of your marriage. Not only are you letting go of your spouse and whatever support and friendship you once enjoyed, but you may be losing ties with your ex-spouse's family members as well, and with some mutual friends. Some of the people who were part of your lives will make a quiet exit, but others will pop up regularly if they live in your neighborhood, if they have children who go to school with yours, or just in the course of everyday life in your town. Having a strategy before a chance meeting can help you feel prepared in the event your paths do cross.

If you have children, your ex-family will expect to continue to be involved in their lives—as well they should. Perhaps their involvement will take place entirely when your ex-spouse has visitation with them, but if you are the custodial parent and your spouse's visitation rights are limited, you can expect your ex's parents, siblings, and others to want to schedule time with your children as well.

Dealing with Your Ex

Earlier in this book, you read about strategies to make your co-parenting relationship with your ex-spouse easier and more comfortable. Many of these ideas carry into your more casual contact with your ex as well—when you see each other at your children's events, in chance meetings in town, or at social occasions. Of course, this is most likely if you both attempt to retain the same social group you enjoyed while you were married. Your friends, not wanting to slight either of you, may invite you both to the same parties and other events. At the very least, you can expect to see each other at friends' weddings, their children's graduations and bar mitzvahs, and other milestone events to which you both should be invited.

If you just can't bear the thought of you and your ex being in the same room, check with him or her by e-mail when you receive an invitation. Don't put your friends in the middle of your divorce—go directly to your ex-spouse and tell him or her that you intend to be at this event, and you want it to be a pleasant day. Give your ex the option of turning down the invitation, or agreeing that there will be no uncomfortable confrontation. This won't serve as a guarantee, but at least you won't be caught off guard.

No matter what your last encounter with your ex was like, you won't gain ground or self-esteem by picking up an old argument or making a snarky remark. Recognize that a chance meeting with your ex is not a reason for your entire personality to change on a dime. If you have not run into each other casually before this, you may feel shock, confusion, panic, and a desire to run in the opposite direction. Even if you do see each other occasionally, you may be taken by surprise and need a few seconds to collect your thoughts. Keep in mind that your ex may be just as flustered as you, and that he or she may not be prepared to deliver a snappy line—or even to say hello. The more quickly you can recover from the shock of seeing your ex, the faster you can take the high ground and set the tone for the conversation.

Divorced Guys LLC has a strong recommendation for this kind of chance meeting. As you're going through the process of beginning your new life as a single person, define yourself with a mission statement and values. What is important to you, and what kind of person do you want to be? Just as your employer may have a mission statement for the company, you need one for yourself. "Over time, memorizing and living your mission statement and your values will make this mental framework flow through your every thought and action," the

Divorced Guys explain. "This reduces and eventually eliminates times of uncertainty."[1]

If you know who you are and what you value, you will know how to respond to your ex's sudden appearance, even if he or she launches into some kind of attack on you as soon as you see each other. If your ex chooses this moment to berate you for a late alimony payment or for sending little Jimmy home with dirty laundry, you can still hold your head high and refuse to escalate the discussion.

Rehearse possible scenarios in your mind and in your mirror before they take place. When the holidays are coming, for example, and you know that you might end up at the same school events with your ex, start thinking about what you will say and how you will turn the conversation if it starts to go sour. You don't need to take the bait that your ex may hurl at you. While he or she may want to start an argument or even make a scene, you are far from obligated to do so. Be friendly and cordial—especially if your children are present—and suggest that you discuss whatever issue is on the table at another time. Tell your ex, "If you really want to talk about this, call me tomorrow when I'm in the office." Any parent will know that "in the office" is code for "when I won't be with the kids."

At some point, one of your chance meetings may involve your ex and his or her new love interest. If you're not seeing anyone yet, this can be a galling experience, especially if you did not know that your ex had started dating again. Such an encounter will probably go one of two ways: (1) the new person will be cordial or even friendly, and will serve as a surprisingly welcome buffer between you and your ex, or (2) the new person will be every bit as uncomfortable as you, and will waste no time extricating himself or herself from the conversation. Either way, meeting the new person will only be as good or bad as you choose to make it. If you perceive the new person to be more attractive, smarter, younger, or richer than you are, you are most likely going to feel miserable about your ex moving on so quickly and beneficially. If the person seems to you to be less attractive, less intelligent, older, or

....

1. Divorced Guys LLC, "Surviving the Holidays: Four Ways to Deal with Ex Wife Run-Ins," YourTango.com, accessed January 17, 2014, http://www.yourtango.com/experts/divorced-guys-llc/surviving-holidays-four-ways-deal-ex-wife-run-ins.

not as successful as you, you may want to gloat to your friends (or you will find yourself thinking, *That's what I've been replaced with? How can that be?*).

No matter how happy you may be with your new life, the discovery that your ex-spouse has moved on can be traumatic. It may bring up old feelings of hurt you thought you'd dismissed, and you may find yourself on the couch with the pint of ice cream again. This time, however, the hurt will be temporary and your new life will demand your attention. Moving on is a good thing for both of you.

Dealing with Mutual Relationships

Relatives who grew to love your spouse or you during your marriage may be completely unsure of how to act around you now that your marriage has ended. Your ex-spouse's family may be uneasy around you, and your ex may have told them things about you that you would prefer they did not know. It's only natural that a person's family will rally around him or her when a long-term relationship ends, so you can expect a difference in the way you interact with them, if you interact with them at all.

If you don't have children, it's entirely possible that your ex's family will never be in contact with you again. They may feel pressure to "divorce" you the way their family member did, out of loyalty to your ex—even if they had a close relationship with you. This can be a big emotional blow, especially if you did not want the divorce and you now feel as though you've lost some of your support system as well as your spouse.

With children in the mix, however, and if you are the custodial parent or your ex's visitation is fairly limited, your ex's family most likely will reach out to you for opportunities to see their grandchildren, nieces, and nephews. They may invite them (and you along with them) to family events, birthday parties with their own kids, and holiday gatherings. Your ex-spouse will most likely be at these events as well.

Grandparents, aunts, and uncles—regardless of which side of the family they come from—give your children love and support, and even financial help if they recognize that this would be appropriate. If they continue to be part of your child's life, they help to establish the kind of stability you want to create for your children. They also show your children that the circumstances that separated their parents do not result in a loss of love for them—an important life lesson that will resonate for years to come. If once-loving grandparents suddenly vanish from your children's lives, the children may develop lowered self-esteem and a sense that they are somehow "damaged goods"—the products of a broken home.

You can establish ground rules for visits from your in-laws, such as the time children need to be in bed and what kinds of gifts you would prefer they not receive, but if the grandparents have a positive influence on the children, there's no reason to screen them out just because your spouse has left the picture. Remember that this part of the relationship is not about you—it's about your children. Do what is in their best interests, just as you promised from the very beginning of your divorce proceeding. There's a practical consideration here as well: Most states have laws that protect the rights of grandparents to see their grandchildren in the event of a divorce. You are legally bound to allow them access, so make it as pleasant and mutually beneficial as you can.[2]

As mentioned briefly earlier, friends can feel uncertain and conflicted about where their loyalties lie once you and your spouse have divorced. Couples who socialized with both of you together may feel they no longer have as much in common with you as a single person. Friends your spouse brought into the relationship probably will remain close to your spouse but may pull back from you over time. Your friends from before your marriage may well do the same.

Generally, the people around your marriage would like to remain neutral, and if they've valued their relationships with both of you, they will attempt to maintain these as long as they feel they're not hurting anyone's feelings. You will have special, lifelong friends to whom you can vent your frustrations and anger at your ex-spouse, friends who have always been there for you and will continue to be during and after

....

2. "Single-Parenting Challenge: Dealing with Former In-Laws," Dummies.com, accessed January 17, 2014, http://www.dummies.com/how-to/content /singleparenting-challenge-dealing-with-former-inla.html.

your divorce. The friends you and your spouse made together, however, may be confused and cautious about what to do now.

You can assist in maintaining these friendships by not venting about your ex-spouse when you are with them, and not discussing your broken marriage if you can avoid doing so. Bringing them your problems with your ex may only make them more uncomfortable, especially if they are trying to maintain a friendship with your ex as well. Try not to create any new drama and strife by bad-mouthing their other friend. Over time, you and your ex may actually manage to move on from your breakup and start to get along again—even to become friends—and all this divisiveness on your part may come back to haunt you.[3]

If being with friends you shared with your spouse is just too painful a reminder of the fun you had with them while you were married, they may not be the friends you will keep for the long term. This may be sad for you, but it also may be necessary to put that relationship aside for the time being. When you have a new love in your life or when you're in a stronger place emotionally, you may want to invite these people back into your life. Chances are they will be pleased that you did.

It is also likely that some of these mutual friends will simply exit your life in favor of maintaining a relationship with your ex. This is their prerogative, and they should not be blamed—they may simply feel they have more in common with your ex-spouse. Even if you fear that your ex has told them things about you to turn them away, you need to let them go. Not everyone wants to play a role in the drama that your life has become, so allow such a couple to bow out, and turn to your close friends for companionship.[4]

....

3. Kristen Moutria, "The Effects of Divorces on Mutual Friendships," GlobalPost .com, accessed January 17, 2014, http://everydaylife.globalpost.com/effects-divorces -mutual-friendships-14139.html.

4. Barton Goldsmith, "After You've Divided Up the Stuff, What about the Friends?," *Psychology Today*, March 4, 2010, http://www.psychologytoday.com/blog/emotional -fitness/201003/after-youve-divided-the-stuff-what-about-the-friends.

Ten Techniques for Dealing with Mutual Relationships

1. **Keep your negative feelings about your spouse to yourself.** You will have a better chance of maintaining friendships for the long term if you don't trash-talk your spouse to your mutual friends. Plus, these are mutual friends—so what's to stop them from repeating the things you say to your ex?

2. **Understand as best you can that some relationships will favor your ex, and some will favor you.** Your best friends will want to stay close to you—not your ex—and the same will be true about his closest friends. Accept the losses as part of the divorce.

3. **Talk to the friends you hope to keep.** Tell them what's going on and what they should expect from you and your ex. This will help them get past the uneasiness they may feel around you, and will give them some guidelines that they can follow.

4. **Make first contact with your ex-parents-in-law.** Tell them that you are open to having them see their grandchildren, and see if they are willing to talk through some guidelines. Chances are they will be very relieved that you got in touch.

5. **Ask your friends to tell you up front if they invite you and your ex to the same event.** You can make the decision about whether to attend without involving them any further.

6. **Don't rush to introduce your new love to your mutual friends.** You may run into resentment from the friends who are loyal to your ex, or they may be predisposed to not like your new love simply because he or she is not your former love. Wait until relationships have stabilized with your friends before you bring your new love into the circle.

7. **Don't blog or post about your ex.** Don't go on Facebook or Twitter and post every little thing that happens throughout your divorce proceeding, or all the things your ex-spouse says or does

that irritate you. Your friends are reading, and this will only make them more uncomfortable.

8. **When your friends bring up your ex, take the high road.** They may try to engage you in trash talk, but don't give in to the temptation. Instead, tell them how glad you are that you had that relationship, because otherwise you would not have met these mutual friends. Then change the subject.

9. **Remember that your friends have suffered a loss, too.** You're not the only one who feels the pain of divorce. Your friends have lost the easy companionship and fun they had with both of you, and in some cases they've lost a friend as well. Respect their feelings, just as you hope they will respect yours.

10. **When you do see your ex, be cordial and polite.** The fastest way to get yourself crossed off the friend list is to make a scene at someone's nice event. Hold your head high and conduct yourself with dignity.

CHAPTER NINE

Moving On

As hard as it can be to believe when you are in the thick of a divorce proceeding, a day will come when the clouds will part and you will begin
to feel like yourself again. All the work you've done to recover from the
effects of a tough breakup will help you lay the groundwork for a new
life for yourself and your children. How you move forward with your
new life will depend on the work you are willing to do to regain your
own self-confidence and self-esteem.

   The process of healing requires a great deal of mental energy and
your willingness to let go of the unanswered questions about your
divorce. Dwelling on the negative forever will not help you reach your
goals for the next phase of your life—in fact, nursing the old anger will
only keep you from moving forward. It's time to find your way out from
under the gray skies to a place where a bright future can replace your
overcast present. You've had a long period of feeling paralyzed by the
slow movement of the legal process, the flood of emotions that come
at the end of a marriage, and the uncertainty of what you will be able
to do next. Now, with your divorce finalized, you can give some serious
thought to what you'd like to do.

Building a New Life

What happens now? That's up to you—but the first thing is to get up,
take a shower, get dressed, and leave the house. The pain of divorce
doesn't end just because you have a signed document from a court, but

you can't just let it go on and on either. Getting up and out may feel nearly impossible, but it has to be done. Keep moving, and soon your momentum will make it easier.

Once you're in motion, you can start making plans. Search within yourself for the answers to some basic questions: Now that you're living independently of your spouse, who are you, and who do you want to be? What kinds of things did you enjoy before you were married? What things might you have given up because your spouse did not share your interest? It's time to re-embrace these activities. This is also a good time to look closely at how you defined yourself during your marriage, and how you will redefine your place in the world now that you are single again.

Having a plan in place can make all the difference in moving from your current position to a new life. It's hard to accomplish an objective if you don't know what that objective is! Setting down your thoughts about where you'd like to be will help you see what steps you should take first and what kind of activity you will need to get there. Of course, setting goals doesn't have to take place all at once, and it doesn't need to be the kind of stiff, formalized process you may have participated in at work. Here is a basic framework to help you get started:

- **Make your wish.** What do you want the end result to be? It could be as simple a statement as "I want to feel better about myself" or "I want to be a good father to my kids," or as complex as "I want to have more fun, make new friends, and visit every state in the country." Already you have more direction than you had when you started.

- **List the challenges.** If you are independently wealthy and you have all kinds of resources at your disposal, you may be able to skip this step. If not, chances are there's something in your current life that you need to deal with as you begin on your journey to achieve your wish. Make a list of these things so you can consider ways to get past these challenges.

- **Define the problem.** Based on what you want and the challenges you have to work with, what problem do you need to solve? Phrase this as a "how" question: "How do I get to travel more on my limited budget?" or "How do I improve my self-image?"

- **Brainstorm.** Generate lots of ideas, and don't worry about whether they are doable or outrageous. Sometimes the best ideas come from outlandish ones—you may not want to become a competitive power lifter, for example, but you could buy a used stationary bike and commit to cardio four or five times a week. Likewise, you may not be able to afford a week at a tropical island spa, but you could talk to your hairdresser about a new style and get a consultation about updating your current look.

- **Winnow the list.** Take a good look at the ideas you've brainstormed, and decide which ones you think are the best. How can you strengthen these? What resources can you bring to bear on turning these ideas into actions? Are some of these ideas completely unworkable at this point, or could they become feasible with some ingenuity and assistance? For example, if one of the ideas involves taking a course or pursuing a degree, what kind of financial aid might be available through the college or community to help you?

- **Make your plan.** Now you have the beginnings of an action plan that will point you toward achieving your initial wish. Which of these items can you do in the short term, and which will take a little longer? Create a timeline and choose something to get started on right away.

You're moving ahead on a plan for your new life, with clear goals and action items to get you there. Even if every item on your list doesn't pan out, you will make changes in your life that will improve your situation, and probably lead you to new friends, new places, and new experiences. Give yourself a pat on the back for getting organized and moving forward!

Dating

How will you know when you're ready to start dating again? Experts all make one point very clear: You need to feel good about yourself before you put yourself back into the dating scene. "Dating is only successful when you're able to show who you really are," writes Ashley Page on MadameNoire.com. "Sadly, a divorce can leave you confused as to who the real you really is. Don't start dating again until you know who you are, inside and out." Above all, Page says, don't be desperate. "There is nothing cute about a woman who is screaming, 'Pick me! Pick me!' . . . Desperation only leads to failed relationships and bad dates. Desperation also leads to settling."[1]

It's a scary thing to start over as a single person, so you're almost certain to feel anxious and self-conscious as you get started—especially if it's been decades since you considered the possibility of seeing someone other than your spouse. You may look at your body in the mirror and think no one will ever want to be seen with you, or you may fear that dating has changed and you don't know what people will expect of you anymore. You may even believe you will be viewed as "damaged goods" now that you're divorced.

Remember that no one will be as critical of how you look, what you say, and how you act as *you* are of yourself. A date will see you in a completely different light from the way your spouse saw you, so whatever hurtful or damaging things your spouse may have told you about your attractiveness or your sex appeal may never enter your date's mind. That being said, divorce can leave you wrung out, bitter, exhausted, and depressed—qualities that are no fun for you and not attractive to a prospective partner. You have work to do on your own self-image before you find yourself sitting over dinner on a first date.

There's no need to rush into finding a new relationship, so take your time—even if you hear that your ex is already dating again. When you feel like you can have a drink with someone and have something to

....

1. Ashley Page, "Rules for Women Dating after Divorce," MadameNoire.com, October 17, 2013, http://madamenoire.com/306250/dating-after-divorce/.

talk about besides a rehash of your entire marriage, you may be ready to reenter the dating scene.

One of the hardest things to remember is that people are not all the same. Yes, you had a bad experience with your spouse, but that does not mean that the experience you have with the next person you meet—or any of the people you meet—will be the same. There are plenty of happy relationships out there, populated by good people who are kind and loving to one another. Your chances of finding one of these are just as good as anyone else's.

Experts agree on this, too: It's time to break your life pattern of the kind of person to whom you're attracted. If you've always chosen flamboyant, loud, flashy people, try dating someone who is quieter and more unassuming. If athletic, competitive people have always been your type, maybe it's time to date someone more laid back with a love of Sunday matinées and small dinner parties. Dating against type can open up a world of new possibilities, including the opportunity to spend time with someone who is not so easily compared with your ex.

Where do you meet single people? It's possible you'll meet someone clubbing, but you'll have a much better opportunity to meet people more like you through activities you enjoy, such as volunteer work, special interest clubs (like a ski club or birding club), or on a legitimate online dating site like Match.com, eHarmony.com, JDate.com, BlackPeopleMeet.com, or ChristianSingles.com. If you're over fifty years old, OurTime.com—a site run by the owner of Match .com—targets people your age and older. SeniorFriendFinder.com, DatingForSeniors.com, and SeniorMatch.com are all geared to an over-fifty crowd, and Match.com itself also provides introductions to older adults. You need to screen your potential dates carefully on these sites, as there are plenty of scammers who use them—but there are lots of good, honest people as well. Tread carefully, but put your best foot forward.

Dating and Children

Take your time before introducing a new love to your children. Remember that there's been a lot of change in your children's lives, and they may not be ready for yet another new variable to be thrust upon them.

Before you insert another adult into your family, make sure that this person is a real keeper, someone who can go the distance with you and your children. If your children like your new love as much as you do, it can be wrenching for them if your relationship goes sour and the new person disappears from their lives. An introduction too soon can also make your children feel that their closeness with you may be threatened, as if you will put your new love's interests above theirs. They may also feel that your new relationship is disloyal to their other parent, even though they know that the two of you are divorced. Children hold out hopes for their parents' reconciliation much longer than you ever will, so the fact that you have moved on can be a tremendous shock.

If they don't like your new romantic partner, their disdain will prey on any low-level uncertainty you may have about the relationship—and the awful thing is that they may see something you don't. Be careful before bringing a new person into your home and giving them a lot of time with your children. Even once you've begun seeing someone special, your number-one priority remains with your children and protecting their health and safety. Do not do anything that might put them in jeopardy.

Ten Tips for Moving On

Beyond general suggestions for ways to approach your new, single life, here are ten actionable ways to work on moving on:

1. **Go ahead and grieve—it's okay.** Unless you were really ready for this divorce, it's unlikely that you will be able to just dust off your hands and think, *Well, that's done*, when your divorce decree arrives and your marriage is officially over. You've experienced a loss as acute as a death in the family, and you need time to feel

mournful and to adjust to a life without your spouse. This will not happen overnight. Give yourself the interval you need to feel the remorse, guilt, and sadness that come with loss.

2. **Learn from the experience and let go of the guilt.** It's a critical part of the healing process, yet many people struggle to stop the cycle of guilt and self-blame that keeps divorced individuals from moving ahead with a new life. You may have made mistakes, but endless self-recrimination will not change the fact of what has happened.

3. **Seek a therapist or life coach.** If you have not already looked into counseling as a way to process your feelings, you may find that you could use assistance in moving past grief. Starting over presents a set of challenges that you may not have foreseen, from the emotional (taking the first steps toward dating) to the practical (learning to use financial software to manage your bank accounts). If the idea of a therapist seems just too touchy-feely for you, consider looking for a professional life coach who can help you examine all aspects of your life ahead.

4. **Remember what you liked before you were married.** Every marriage involves compromise, so it's likely that you forfeited some favorite activity when you married your ex-spouse. What did you enjoy before? Maybe you had a passion for Asian cooking, or fine wine, or racquetball, or hip-hop dancing. You may have loved camping and nature hikes, but your spouse hated sleeping on the ground; perhaps you loved opera, but your spouse didn't appreciate classical music. You may have left your religious affiliation behind in favor of your spouse's faith, or perhaps you have not been to a live sporting event since you were married. Whatever you gave up, embrace it again. It may come with a whole social life you had forgotten existed.

5. **Make a plan.** When you commit your thoughts to a document, they become much more real and you are more likely to accomplish them. List all the things you would like to do, from fixing the window shades in the den to getting a master's degree. Prioritize

these goals according to what you can do right away, what will take time, and what will be important for the long term.

6. **Unclutter.** Not just around the house but throughout your relationships and your daily schedule, there are things that you simply don't need to own or do anymore—and things you don't want to do as well. If you've been volunteering at your spouse's place of worship, you may feel no need to continue this. If you're the captain of the carpool, it may be time to pass that baton to another parent in the mix. Your new life will be complex enough without adding obligations that don't bring you joy or value. This is a good time to clear some of this stuff out of your life.

7. **Try something new.** Maybe you've always wanted to try hang gliding, or you crave the stimulation and camaraderie of a book club, or you really want to learn to make sushi. Hook yourself up with a class or a Groupon for something you would love to try out. Who knows, you might even make some new friends in the process.

8. **Keep a journal.** You don't need to handwrite it in a blank book, but having the conversation with yourself on paper or on the computer screen can give you a ready outlet for anything you feel, from rage to sorrow to joy. Julia Cameron, author of *The Artist's Way* and a number of other books on creativity, recommends that every person spends time first thing in the morning writing three pages of a journal to get all the baggage and harsh feelings out of your system before you begin your day. These "morning pages" serve to clear your head of the doubts, fears, guilt, anger, and any other emotions before you step out the door, leaving them behind and allowing you to be more effective as the day goes on.[2]

9. **Make new, single friends.** As covered in chapter 8, one of the toughest things to get past in your healing process is the fact that all your friends see you as part of a couple, and they don't

....

2. Julia Cameron, *The Artist's Way: A Spiritual Path to Higher Creativity* (New York: Jeremy P. Tarcher/Putnam, 1992).

know how to respond to you as a single person. New friends will know only the person you present to them today, so they have no preconceived ideas about you that interfere with the person you'd like to become. You will be more comfortable with people who are single and having the same kinds of life experiences that you are now.

10. **Take a trip.** What better time to get away to see a foreign land than at a time in your life when everything is changing? You have been through an ordeal and come out on the other side, and you deserve a celebration. If your finances allow it, team up with a group of friends and take a getaway cruise or a tour of the wineries of France—or the vineyards of California or the New York Finger Lakes if that's a more affordable choice. The break will help you focus on something other than the upheaval in your life, and you will come home refreshed and energized.[3]

....

3. Norine Dworkin-McDaniel, "Life after Divorce: 12 Ways to Rebuild Your Life," LifeScript.com, December 12, 2011, http://www.lifescript.com/life/relationships /wreckage/12_ways_to_heal_from_divorce.aspx.

Conclusion

There is life after your marriage, even though it may seem like you will never feel normal again. A day will come when you can put the past behind you and return to a life of meaningful, productive activity—when you can give yourself permission to be happy once again.

This book provides you with the starting points to help you find your way through your divorce and what follows. Even if you come out in pieces on the other side of the trauma, with the right tools and the right outlook, you can put yourself and your life back together. Do it soon. You won't enjoy your time of self-blame and self-pity, and you are not meant to linger there.

Just like every person on this planet, you are entitled to life, liberty, and the pursuit of happiness—no matter what mistakes you have made or what you may feel you have done to deserve so much pain. You may find yourself going through the motions at first, but after a time, your attempts to return to normalcy will become more genuine and you may even find that you can function again—even happily.

Glossary

abandonment: The willful forsaking or forgoing of parental duties. If one spouse abandons the other and there are children involved, this is considered a criminal act in most states.

alimony: Monetary support given to the lower-earning spouse by the higher-earning spouse for a period of time determined by the divorce proceeding.

annulment: A legal decree that states the marriage never occurred.

arbitration: A divorce process in which the spouses meet with a private judge who acts as an arbitrator, and agree before the proceeding begins to accept his or her decision on the case.

assets: Useful or valuable things that you own.

at-fault: A divorce in which one spouse has created an intolerable situation for the other, which includes such actions as infidelity, physical or psychological abuse, desertion, alcohol or drug addiction, gambling addiction, or commission of a crime.

beneficiary: A person designated in a will, on a life insurance policy, or on a bank account to receive the proceeds in the case of the owner's death.

child support: Required payments from the noncustodial parent to the custodial parent to share the children's living expenses. These usually include food, clothing, shelter, and medical, health, and education expenses.

collaborative divorce: A divorce that involves specially trained attorneys who work cooperatively with both spouses to settle the case.

community property: Assets earned by the two spouses are owned by both of them. Arizona, California, Idaho, Louisiana, Nevada, New Mexico, Texas, Washington, and Wisconsin are all community-property states.

consanguinity: A close relationship by blood or law (marrying your natural brother, your adopted brother, or your stepbrother, for example).

contested: You and your spouse cannot agree on one or more issues, and must appear in court to have a judge order a solution.

conversion divorce: A conversion of a legal separation agreement to a divorce.

countersuit: A lawsuit filed in response to a lawsuit to accuse the accuser and undo or reduce the impact of the original suit.

custodial parent: The parent with whom the children actually live for more than 50 percent of the time. The custodial parent is the primary parent in the divorce relationship.

custody: The protective care of something or someone; in divorce, this most often refers to the parent who has primary care for the children.

default divorce: A divorce granted when one of the spouses cannot be found or fails to respond to the divorce petition.

desertion: Abandonment of a spouse without just cause, including the failure to provide care for a spouse who is in ill health or otherwise unable to provide for him or herself.

diriment impediment: An impairment in one of the spouses that should have prevented the marriage from taking place.

dissolution: A fast divorce in which both spouses agree upfront about child custody, parental rights, visitation, support, division of property, and payment of fees.

equitable distribution: A law that means that the property you acquired during the marriage belongs to you, and the property your spouse acquired belongs to your spouse. In a divorce, the property is divided in as fair and equitable a manner as possible. All but nine U.S. states use equitable distribution.

executor: A person designated in a will to execute the will according to the wishes of the deceased.

grounds: The legally acceptable reason that you want your marriage to end.

irreconcilable differences or **irretrievable breakdown:** An inability of two spouses to tolerate living together, and an agreement that the relationship cannot be repaired.

legal custody: Authorization by the court to make decisions about the overall health and welfare of a child.

legal separation: A court order that permits two spouses to live apart while they are still legally married.

litigation: Engaging in legal proceedings to settle a disagreement.

mediator: A neutral third party who is trained to assist with communication and negotiation between the two spouses.

no-fault: Neither party needs to prove that the other has done anything wrong to proceed with a divorce.

noncustodial parent: The parent with whom the children do not live, or with whom they live less than 50 percent of the time.

petition: A document filed by one or both spouses requesting that the court grant a divorce.

petitioner: The spouse who files the divorce petition.

physical custody: The parent(s) with whom the children live at least 50 percent of the time.

process server: A person over eighteen years old who can deliver the petition to the respondent.

property: Just about anything you and your spouse own, from physical items to bank accounts.

pro se: Someone who represents himself or herself in court, without an attorney.

protective order: A court order that forbids one spouse from entering the home or coming into contact with the children or other spouse.

raptus: In the Catholic church, the abduction of someone with the intention of marrying him or her.

residency requirement: The requirement that you live in a state or county for a certain period of time before you can file for divorce there.

respondent: The spouse who receives the divorce petition from the petitioner.

restraining order: A court order that prevents a specific action on the part of the person ordered. This action may be a prohibition against using marital assets, visiting the children, or coming within a set distance of the other spouse.

subpoena: A summons ordering a person to attend a court.

substantial competent evidence: Tangible proof that one parent is not fit to serve in a specific capacity, most often as a custodial parent.

summary divorce: A simple divorce granted when the marriage lasted for fewer than five years, there are no children, the couple does not own a house or any other real property, and each spouse's personal property is worth less than a threshold set by the state.

uncontested: The spouses agree on all aspects of the divorce settlement without the use of attorneys.

visitation: Scheduled time in which the noncustodial parent can spend time with the children.

Divorce Resources

- **AllLaw.com:** A law portal with information on many issues, including divorce, family law, and child custody.

- **ChildrenandDivorce.com:** Divorce resources for parents, professionals, and children.

- **Cornell University Law School Legal Information Institute (www.law.cornell.edu/wex/divorce):** This venerable law school's website provides consumer-level information on various legal matters.

- **DadsDivorce.com:** Resources specifically for fathers going through a divorce.

- **DivorceOnline.com:** Navigate to www.divorceonline.com/state -divorce-laws/ and click on the link for your state to find detailed pages on your local divorce laws.

- **DivorceResourceCenter.com:** For people facing an unwanted divorce.

- **DivorceSource.com:** This site's landing page provides links to information about every state's divorce laws and requirements.

- **DivorceSupport.com:** Forums and resources for the divorced and to-be divorced.

- **FindLaw.com:** The dictionary page on this website (dictionary .findlaw.com/legal-glossary/divorce-and-family-law.html) provides quick definitions to many of the terms you will hear used by your attorney or the court system.

- **LawyerLocator.com:** This site provides basic information on divorce law and a search function to help you find a divorce attorney in your community.

- **MyDivorcePapers.com:** A series of videos on this site can help you understand how the law will affect specific issues, including distribution of retirement-plan funds, debt, real estate, other property, child support, and many others.

- **Nolo.com:** One of the web's largest libraries of legal information for consumers.

- **Pace University Law School Women's Justice Center (www.law.pace.edu/divorce-q):** This site provides a detailed question-and-answer page on divorce, with links to the responses that are of greatest interest to you.

References

Benson, Lisa A., Meghan M. McGinn, and Andrew Christensen. "Common Principles of Couple Therapy." *Behavior Therapy* 43, no. 1 (March 2012): 25–35. doi:10.1016/j.beth.2010.12.009.

Bishop, Susan. "Should You Move Out of the Family Home during a Divorce?" DivorceNet.com. Accessed January 8, 2014. http://www.divorcenet.com /resources/divorce/marital-property-division/should-you-move-out-family-hom.

Block, Jocelyn, and Melinda Smith. "Tips for Divorced Parents: Co-parenting with Your Ex and Making Joint Custody Work." Helpguide.org. Last modified December 2013. http://www.helpguide.org/mental/coparenting_shared _parenting_divorce.htm.

Braselton, Debra J. "Ten Things You Need to Do If Divorce Is Imminent." Family -Law-Illinois.com. Accessed January 14, 2014. http://www.family-law-illinois .com/Divorce/Things-You-Need-To-Do-If-Divorce-Is-Imminent.shtml.

CADivorce.com. "How Will the Court Decide My Child Custody Case?" Accessed January 15, 2014. http://www.cadivorce.com/california-divorce-guide /child-custody-and-visitation/how-will-the-court-decide-my-child-custody-case/.

Cameron, Julia. *The Artist's Way: A Spiritual Path to Higher Creativity.* New York: Jeremy P. Tarcher/Putnam, 1992.

CatholicDoors.com. "Frequently Asked Questions about Reasons/Grounds for Obtaining a Marriage Annulment." Last modified September 3, 2011. http:// www.catholicdoors.com/faq/qu79.htm.

Champlin, Joseph M. "Ten Questions about Annulment." *Catholic Update.* October 2002. http://www.americancatholic.org/newsletters/cu/ac1002.asp.

Collingwood, Jane. "Reduce the Stress of a Divorce." PsychCentral.com. Accessed January 16, 2014. http://psychcentral.com/lib/reduce-the-stress-of-a -divorce/0001003.

Divorced Guys LLC. "Surviving the Holidays: Four Ways to Deal with Ex Wife Run- Ins." YourTango.com. Accessed January 17, 2014. http://www.yourtango.com /experts/divorced-guys-llc/surviving-holidays-four-ways-deal-ex-wife-run-ins.

DivorceNet.com. "How to Protect Yourself during Divorce." Accessed January 8, 2014. http://www.divorcenet.com/states/california/steps_to_protect_yourself _during_divorce.

DivorceSupport.com. "Picking a Divorce Lawyer." Accessed January 9, 2014. http:// www.divorcesupport.com/divorce/Picking-a-Divorce-Lawyer-2942.html.

DivorceSupport.com. "Preparing Your Divorce Lawyer Checklist." Accessed January 9, 2014. http://www.divorcesupport.com/divorce/Preparing-Your -Divorce-Lawyer-Checklist-2944.html.

Dummies.com. "Single-Parenting Challenge: Dealing with Former In-Laws." Accessed January 17, 2014. http://www.dummies.com/how-to/content /singleparenting-challenge-dealing-with-former-inla.html.

Dworkin-McDaniel, Norine. "Life after Divorce: 12 Ways to Rebuild Your Life." LifeScript.com. December 12, 2011. http://www.lifescript.com/life /relationships/wreckage/12_ways_to_heal_from_divorce.aspx.

Emma, Linda. "How to Get Over Hating Your Ex-Spouse." ModernMom.com. Accessed January 14, 2014. http://motherhood.modernmom.com/over-hating -exspouse-8489.html.

Experian.com. "Getting Removed as Joint Credit Card Account Holder." Accessed January 13, 2014. http://www.experian.com/blogs/ask-experian/2013/02/28 /getting-removed-as-joint-credit-card-account-holder/.

FamilyLives.org.uk. "Dealing with Stress and Depression during Divorce and Separation." Accessed January 16, 2014. http://familylives.org.uk/advice /divorce-and-separation/thinking-about-divorce/dealing-with-stress-and -depression-during-divorce-and-separation/.

FedLawBoston.com. "How to Protect Your Assets in the Event of a Divorce."
Accessed January 10, 2014. http://www.feldlawboston.com/Family-Law/How
-To-Protect-Assets-in-Divorce.aspx.

FindLaw.com. "Divorce and Property." Accessed January 10, 2014. http://family
.findlaw.com/divorce/divorce-property.html?DCMP=GOO-FAM_Divorce
-Property&HBX_PK=divorce+property+rights.

FindLaw.com. "Divorce Property Division FAQ." Accessed January 10, 2014.
http://family.findlaw.com/divorce/divorce-property-division-faq.html.

FindLaw.com. "Inheritance and Divorce." Accessed January 13, 2014. http://
family.findlaw.com/divorce/inheritance-and-divorce.html.

Goldsmith, Barton. "After You've Divided Up the Stuff, What about the Friends?"
Psychology Today. March 4, 2010. http://www.psychologytoday.com/blog
/emotional-fitness/201003/after-youve-divided-the-stuff-what-about-the-friends.

Guillen, Lina. "15 Critical Mistakes in Divorce." DivorceNet.com. Accessed
January 14, 2014. http://www.divorcenet.com/states/new_york/15_critical
_mistakes_in_divorce.

Herron, Janna. "Close Credit Card Accounts in Divorce." Bankrate.com. Accessed
January 13, 2014. http://www.bankrate.com/finance/credit-cards/close-credit
-card-accounts-divorce.aspx.

Kemp, Gina, Melinda Smith, and Jeanne Segal. "Children and Divorce: Helping
Kids Cope with Separation and Divorce." Helpguide.org. Last modified
December 2013. http://www.helpguide.org/mental/children_divorce.htm.

Kübler-Ross, Elisabeth. *On Death and Dying: What the Dying Have to Teach
Doctors, Nurses, Clergy, and Their Own Families*. New York: Scribner
Classics, 1997.

LaMance, Ken. "Automatic Restraining Order." LegalMatch.com. Accessed
January 9, 2014. http://www.legalmatch.com/law-library/article/automatic
-restraining-order.html.

———. "Emergency Protective Orders." LegalMatch.com. Accessed January 9, 2014.
http://www.legalmatch.com/law-library/article/emergency-protective
-orders.html.

Landers, Jeffrey A. "9 Critical Steps Women Should Take to Prepare for Divorce." *Huffington Post*. March 3, 2011. http://www.huffingtonpost.com/jeffrey-a -landers/9-critical-steps-women-sh_b_828841.html.

LegalZoom.com. "Child Support in a Divorce." Accessed February 3, 2014. http:// www.legalzoom.com/divorce-guide/divorce-child-support.html.

LegalZoom.com. "Comparing Equitable Distribution and Community Property for a Divorce." Accessed January 8, 2014. http://www.legalzoom.com/divorce -guide/equitable-distribution-community-property.html.

LegalZoom.com. "Custody of Minor Children in a Divorce." Accessed January 15, 2014. http://www.legalzoom.com/divorce-guide/custody-of-minor-children .html.

Lewis, Jennifer, and William Sammons. "Looking at Divorce—Through the Eyes of a Child." ChildrenandDivorce.com. Accessed January 15, 2014. http://www .childrenanddivorce.com/id18.html.

MacDonald, Ann. "How Do Family Courts Split Up Debt upon Divorce?" LegalZoom.com. Accessed January 13, 2014. http://www.legalzoom.com /marriage-divorce-family-law/divorce/how-do-family-courts-split.

Markham, Laura. "Divorce: Protecting Your Kids." AhaParenting.com. January 15, 2014. http://www.ahaparenting.com/parenting-tools/family-life /Divorce-protecting-kids.

Meyer, Cathy. "How Do the Courts Determine Alimony?" About.com. Divorce Support. Accessed January 13, 2014. http://divorcesupport.about.com/od /financialissues/f/alimonyconsider.htm.

———. "How to Negotiate the Best Possible Settlement." About.com. Divorce Support. Accessed January 14, 2014. http://divorcesupport.about.com/od /propertydistribution/ht/divagreement.htm.

———. "Pro Se Divorce Litigation, Obtaining a Divorce without an Attorney." About .com. Divorce Support. Accessed January 9, 2014. http://divorcesupport.about .com/od/yourlegalrights/a/pro_se.htm.

_____. "The Emotional Stages of Divorce: What to Expect during and after the Divorce Process." *Huffington Post*. November 8, 2010. http://www.huffingtonpost.com/cathy-meyer/the-emotional-stages-of-d_b_779816.html.

_____. "Top 5 Things to Consider When Hiring a Divorce Attorney." About.com. Divorce Support. Accessed January 9, 2014. http://divorcesupport.about.com/od/hiringtherightattorney/tp/rightattorney.htm.

Moutria, Kristen. "The Effects of Divorces on Mutual Friendships." GlobalPost.com. Accessed January 17, 2014. http://everydaylife.globalpost.com/effects-divorces-mutual-friendships-14139.html.

NationalParalegal.edu. "Fault vs. No-Fault Divorce." Accessed January 8, 2014. http://nationalparalegal.edu/public_documents/courseware_asp_files/domesticRelations/Divorce/FaultVsNoFaultDivorce.asp.

NNEDV.org. "US State and Territorial Coalitions." Accessed February 3, 2014. http://nnedv.org/resources/coalitions.html.

Nolo.com. "Child Custody and Religion." Accessed January 15, 2014. http://www.nolo.com/legal-encyclopedia/child-custody-religion-29887.html.

Nolo.com. "Dividing Property and Debt during Divorce FAQ." Accessed January 15, 2014. http://www.nolo.com/legal-encyclopedia/dividing-property-debt-during-divorce-faq-29127.html.

Nolo.com. "Divorce: Do You Need a Lawyer?" Accessed January 9, 2014. http://www.nolo.com/legal-encyclopedia/divorce-do-you-need-lawyer-29502.html.

Nolo.com. "Searching for Hidden Assets at Divorce." Accessed January 10, 2014. http://www.nolo.com/legal-encyclopedia/searching-hidden-assets-divorce-29968.html.

Nolo.com. "Temporary Orders in Family Court: Quick Decisions on Support and Custody." Accessed January 15, 2014. http://www.nolo.com/legal-encyclopedia/temporary-orders-family-court-29642.html.

Page, Ashley. "Rules for Women Dating after Divorce." MadameNoire.com. October 17, 2013. http://madamenoire.com/306250/dating-after-divorce/.

U.S. Census Bureau. "Marriages and Divorces—Number and Rate by State: 1990 to 2009." Table 133 in *Statistical Abstract of the United States: 2012*. http://www.census.gov/compendia/statab/2012/tables/12s0133.pdf.

Warner, Debra. "7 Steps to Overcome Your Divorce." PBS. *This Emotional Life* (blog). Accessed January 10, 2014. http://www.pbs.org/thisemotionallife/blogs/7-steps-overcome-your-divorce.

WomensFinance.com. "Divorce: Alimony Payments." Accessed January 13, 2014. http://www.womensfinance.com/wf/divorce/alimony1.asp.

Whitbourne, Susan Krauss. "5 Principles of Effective Couples Therapy." *Psychology Today*. March 20, 2012. http://www.psychologytoday.com/blog/fulfillment-any-age/201203/5-principles-effective-couples-therapy.

Wynns, Kristen. "Dealing with Divorce: 10 Tips to Protect Your Kids." WynnsFamilyPsychology.com. Accessed January 15, 2014. http://wynnsfamilypsychology.com/DealingwithDivorce10TipstoProtectYourKids/tabid/760/language/en-US/Default.aspx.

Index

making agreement
with, on priority of
children, 83
not blogging or posting
about, 106–107
speaking directly with, 70

F

Family
quid pro quo with, 95
withdrawal from, 66
Financial checklist, 57–58
Financial records, getting in
order, 7
FindLaw.com, 26, 123
Fitness for parenthood, 76
Force, civil annulment and, 20
Forgiving and letting go, 98
Friends
asking about inviting
spouse to same
event, 106
bring up ex-spouse by, 107
loss of, 107
making new single,
115–116
making plans with, 95
quid pro quo with, 95
talking with those you
hope to keep, 106
withdrawal from, 67

G

Gifts, surprise, 50
Grades, falling, 66
Grieving, 113–114
Grounds, 14, 120
Guilt, 114

H

Health insurance, in
negotiating a settlement
agreement, 56
Home-equity line of credit, 16
House
cleaning and uncluttering,
65, 98, 115
moving out of, 11–12, 31

in negotiating a settlement
agreement, 56
silence around the, 67

I

Incest, annulment and, 10, 20
Income
lack of spouse earning, 11
versus lifestyle, 50
Information, collecting, on
spouse, 8
Inheritance, protecting, 46–47
Insomnia, 67
Internet, getting divorce on
the, 10
Intoxication, civil annulment
and, 20
Inventory, taking, 31
Investments, 29–30
Irreconcilable differences
as grounds for divorce,
15, 120
Irretrievable breakdown, 120

J

JDate.com, 112
Joint (or shared) legal
custody, 77
Joint (or shared) physical
custody, 77, 78
Journal, keeping, 115

K

Kübler-Ross, Elisabeth, 91–92

L

LawyerLocator.com, 26, 123
Lawyers. See Attorney
Legal custody, 120
Legal rights, understanding
your, 28–30
Legal separation, 9, 19–20, 120
Life, building a new, 108–110
Life coach, seeking a, 114
Life script, closing, 98
Lifestyle, income versus, 50
Litigation, 120
costs of, 38

Living will, changing your, 7–8
Lump-sum settlement, 53–54

M

MadameNoire.com, 111
Marital home, access to, 43
Marital property versus your
property, 43–44
Marriage
length of, 54
standard of living during
the, 54
Match.com, 112
Mediated divorce, 25
Mediator, 33, 120
Misrepresentation, civil
annulment and, 20
Money, being closed-mouth
about, 50
Moving on, 108–116
building new life, 108–110
dating in, 111–113
tips for, 113–116
Moving out of house, 11–12, 31
Mutual relationships, dealing
with, 103–107
MyDivorcePapers.com, 26, 123

N

No-fault divorce, 9, 15, 24, 120
Nolo.com, 27, 123
Noncustodial parent, 120

O

On Death and Dying (Kübler-
Ross), 91–92
Order to show cause (OSC),
74–75

P

Pace University Law School
Women's Justice Center,
27, 123
Page, Ashley, 111
Papers
making copies of
important, 31
signing of, 31, 50

Notes

Notes